For dear friends and teammates around the world who have a burning passion for Jesus and for sport.

BRYAN MASON
BEYOND THE
GOLD

WHAT EVERY CHURCH NEEDS TO KNOW ABOUT SPORTS MINISTRY

Authentic

Copyright © 2011 Bryan Mason

23 22 21 20 19 18 17   8 7 6 5 4 3 2

First published 2011 by Authentic Media Limited
PO Box 6326, Bletchley, Milton Keynes, MK1 9GG
www.authenticmedia.co.uk

Reprinted 2017

Some of the material in this book has previously been published in *Into the Stadium* by Bryan Mason © 2003 by Spring Harvest and Authentic Media.

British Library Cataloguing in Publication Data
A catalogue record for this book is available from the British Library
ISBN 978-1-86024-811-5

Unless otherwise marked, Scripture quotations are taken from
THE HOLY BIBLE, NEW INTERNATIONAL VERSION.
Copyright © 1973, 1978, 1984 by Biblica. Used by permission of
Hodder & Stoughton Publishers, a member of the Hachette Livre UK
Group. All rights reserved.
Scripture quotations marked '*The Message*' are taken from *The Message*
copyright © 1993, 1994, 1995, 1996, 2000, 2001, 2002. Used by permission
of NavPress Publishing Group.
Scripture quotations marked 'CEV' are taken from Contemporary
English Version copyright © 1995 American Bible Society. All rights
reserved.

Cover design by Paul Airy at DesignLeft (www.designleft.co.uk)
Printed and bound by CPI Group (UK) Ltd, Croydon, CR0 4YY

FOREWORD

The person who came up with the saying that 'Christians never retire' must have done so after spending a day with Bryan Mason. There has rarely been a man with such energy to burn in sharing the gospel in the world of sport. When I first met him about twenty years ago, he was on the point of taking early retirement from being deputy head teacher of a large Yorkshire comprehensive school, in order to spend more time in evangelism. On doing so, he spent nine years working with local churches across the UK on behalf of Christians in Sport. After this time, he still couldn't resist the offer to become European Director for the American-based Church Sports and Recreation Ministers organization (CSRM). After a hugely committed five years in that role, it appeared he might finally slow down and put his feet up. However, the advent of the 2012 London Olympics and his vision for a new sports mission strategy, which he called Higher Sports, meant that the new challenge demanded delaying the pipe and slippers once again.

This book is, therefore, the product of fifteen years of formal sports ministry experience, as well as at least twenty-five more years spent informally in evangelism and discipleship to sportspeople through the local church. It offers a panoramic view of the possibilities and pitfalls of sports ministry and does so with a clear passion and commitment for the local church; it is written in a way that both informs and challenges the reader. I am confident that anyone who reads *Beyond the Gold* will be encouraged that the local church can only gain from being involved in mission to their sports community. I'm glad that Christians never retire!

Graham Daniels
General Director, Christians in Sport

ACKNOWLEDGEMENTS

The international sports ministry family is a remarkable team. Any conversation with this delightful group of people that are so passionate about their love for Jesus and sport can lead to many an inspired vision and serendipity. Since a God-incidental meeting with Graham Daniels, General Director of Christians in Sport, in the early 90s, my path has been strewn with Christian sportsmen and women whom I look forward to sharing heaven with.

Loughborough University must be given the first credit for the unfettered enthusiasm it gave me for every kind of sport. As well as continuing to be the torchbearer for sports science in the United Kingdom and, arguably, in the world, it was also the location for the start of my Christian life as a 19-year-old student. I still continue to enjoy membership of Loughborough's outstanding Alumni Association.

There is insufficient space in this section to acknowledge all those who will have fuelled the forthcoming chapters but mention must be made of the following 'big-hitters'.

The Reverend Andrew Wingfield Digby was the first General Director of Christians in Sport who, together with Graham Daniels and Stuart Weir, appointed me to my first full-time sports ministry position after thirty years of teaching in state schools. Stuart has now moved on to be the Executive Director of Verité Sport and continues to have a huge impact internationally through his writing and personal ministry at the highest sporting level.

Beyond these shores, five Americans stand out as cornerstones in twentieth- and twenty-first-century sports ministry: Dr Greg Linville, Professor at Malone University in Canton, Ohio, for his deep friendship and world expertise in the area of local church sports ministry; Dr Steve Connor, Executive Director of Sports Outreach and former Chicago Bears line-backer, for his pioneering and groundbreaking work in the area of youth sports camp in the UK; Rodger Oswald, Executive Director of Church Sports International, as the man who played a huge part in mentoring me during my early days in sports ministry; Steve Quatro, Professor at Azuza Pacific University in Los Angeles, who helped me understand what being a 'buddy in Christ' was all about; and finally Eddie Waxer, the driving force behind the International Sports Coalition, whose impetus and faithfulness has given rise to countless sports ministry ventures around the world.

To quote the words of Henry V on the eve of the Battle of Agincourt, the above guys have a secure place among my 'happy few'.

PROLOGUE

In his final moments on earth, Jesus asked his followers to 'go and make disciples of all nations' (Matthew 28:19). I believe that the greatest conduit in the twenty-first century for this ageless commission is the one offered by sport and recreation.

The author has been privileged to see the sports ministry gospel change lives all around the world with the good news of Jesus. Many observations and experiences of those times are included in these pages, together with a host of practical examples for the novice and seasoned practitioner alike to implement in a church and community setting. The strategies and programmes outlined are not the domain solely of the highly skilled sportsman or woman and neither are they tied to any particular age group or gender. They will, however, come into their own when in the hands of those with a passion for Jesus and sport, in that order.

If you have an enjoyment for sport, enjoy being with people and want to share what living for Jesus is all about then there will be much in these pages to get your teeth into. At a time when the world is besotted with podiums and prizes, the message from heaven points us to that place 'beyond the gold'.

CONTENTS

INTRODUCTION

It was the occasion of my 400 metres assessment run at Loughborough and I'd started the day with the recommended piece of dry toast and small cup of tea – how things have changed in the world of athletic preparation! My athletics coach wasn't one for long speeches and never wasted words. His pithy statement that morning has remained fixed in my mind ever since: 'Always run beyond the tape and remember that the winner is the one that slows down the least.'

As the 2012 London Olympics approaches and the countless international events that follow, there will be a lot of talk about winning medals and trophies. For the Christian sports-minded person the key is always to see 'beyond the tape', a theme picked up by the Apostle Paul when he speaks of the Christian faith being of 'greater worth than gold' (1 Peter 1:7).

The Olympic ideal of 'it's not the winning it's the taking part' suffered a bit of a bashing when my son Ben was a 14-year-old rugby player. On his bedroom door he had a photo of the pugilistic English rugby hooker, Brian Moore, as he came off the field at Twickenham following an encounter with the French. The caption below his muddy features and scattered locks read 'It's not the winning it's the taking a-part!' Competition certainly brings out the best and the worst but is a place where God wants to feature.

The local church has a vital part to play in our sports-mad world. That part is to bring heaven down onto the playing fields, around the track, into the gymnasium, on the golf course and wherever people meet to enjoy themselves in sporting pursuits. One thing is for certain, no one else is doing it! To play sport and be involved in recreation has its fulfilment when those involved appreciate the gifts and enjoyment God has given them, allowing it to come through in their determination, effort and attitude to those around. To simply aim for the tape is to risk falling short of the mark.

In all walks of life we learn most from those who are role modelling the journey we want to take. Like me, you can probably recall many who have fitted this description and helped you along the way. However, for the Christian sportsperson the first port of call must always be Jesus, the ultimate role model.

Jesus 'Playing Away'

The church in recent times has become too comfortable in its own patch. Much occupied with tending the wounded in the first aid tent, it has forgotten that there is a war on and that both new ground needs to be taken and old ground reclaimed. The forces of darkness have captured many an outpost and, in a world of shrinking absolutes, humankind has trouble distinguishing right from wrong.

If the church is to become the centre of people's lives again and their temperature gauge for godly living, then it must venture forth from its 'home' ground and be prepared to 'play away' at regular intervals. Sport offers a great stage for the Christian life to blossom and grow as it interacts with those of all creeds, cultures and customs. This is where the lifestyle and vision of Jesus comes into its own.

Jesus did not take up a 'synagogue stance' and wait for needy people to join him there. He spent his earthly life 'playing away'. The week might start with him defying culture as he sat by a well with a woman of questionable character. It was, however, a situation that changed the woman of Samaria's life for eternity and brought spiritual revival to her village. Not a bad 'away' result for the Kingdom of God. The following day may have found him speaking to a capacity crowd on a grassy knoll overlooking Lake Galilee. Many would have been delighted that day because the Son of God came onto their turf, and who knows how many other lives were changed because of that day's work? The religious representatives would have then become apoplectic at the sight of Jesus disappearing into the red light district of the time in order to extend the love of God to Mary Magdalene in a church 'no go' area.

With Jesus as the role model for 'playing away' the church should be inspired to follow his example. In this respect, there is an ideal opportunity for those with a passion for Jesus and sport. This spiritual and physical combination is probably the best-kept secret in Christendom. The purpose of this book is to uncover this secret and provide the twenty-first-century sports disciple with a thrilling opportunity to extend the Kingdom of God by reaching the lost with the good news of salvation in Christ.

It is my contention that sport is as vital a part of the church programme as, say, youth work or women's ministry. Indeed, by its all encompassing nature, it reaches out to every age group. As we move on in a century that will shortly see the over-50s age group become one-third of the population in the UK, the church needs to have a dynamic strategy towards both young and old and an appropriate programme to suit both. Sport and recreation can meet these criteria at every level, from children to the active retired. Later in the book there will be a closer examination of different age groups and a teasing out of the activities to suit each one in turn.

Finally, the emphasis in any local church's sport and recreation programme must be on outreach. The one-off meeting with the well-known sports personality, which may well attract a capacity crowd of course, is not genuine sports ministry unless it is crafted around a regular ongoing schedule and is equally sensitive to the personality being exposed. The ideal scenario is the creation of a situation where people enjoy the company and the activity and Jesus can be talked about as naturally as the sports results from the previous day. Research continues to reveal the high percentage of people who become Christians due to the influence of a Christian friend. Sport is such an ideal atmosphere for making friends and sharing the difference Jesus Christ makes in your life. It is arguably the greatest door of opportunity in the post-modern world for the church to grow. As you read this book and put its ideas into practice, it is my hope and prayer that your own church will grow significantly.

Jesus can be talked about as naturally as the sports results from the previous day

1

FIRM
FOOTINGS

Remember, there is only one foundation, the one already laid:
Jesus Christ

1 Corinthians 3:11 (*The Message*)

Open Doors

I have spent some time in Russia working with Russian
churches and seeking to convince them of the viability and
potential of sport and recreation ministry in a land still in
turmoil but open to the life-changing qualities of the gospel.
Unfortunately, the Russian pastors remember too much of
the abuse of sport under communism prior to 1991 and find
it hard to believe that sport and recreation can have any spiritual benefit. The church that had banned one of its members
for jogging in his spare time would be firmly in this camp, as
would the USSR 50 kilometre cycling champion of the 1980s
that I met at a Baptist conference in Bryansk. Since becoming
a Christian, he had not got back on his bike and described his
only feeling of euphoria in all his years of cycling as lasting
about thirty seconds. That was when he stood on the podi-
um to receive his medal. The rest he recalled as a waste of
time when he was a slave to the idol of sport and the
demands of the State. I am pleased to say that the resultant
conversations, and later email correspondence that we had,

served to reveal to Vladimir the incredible gifting he had received from God and how he could use it to glorify his Creator and communicate the good news of Jesus. The church militant in Russia is at a very exciting stage, and the following biblical foundations and apologetics of sports ministry are as much for them as for the British and American church.

Definition

It is important that we define and describe sports ministry before we seek to defend it as part of the plans and purposes of God. Sport is a comprehensive and inclusive term that identifies a vast array of activities with varying degrees of intensity and competition. In his book *More Than Champions*, Stuart Weir records the findings of the Council of Europe and Sport England:

Sport means all forms of physical activity, which through casual or organized participation, aim at expressing or improving physical fitness and mental well-being, forming social relationships or obtaining results in competition at all levels. (Council of Europe)

Sport England categorizes sport into four areas:

1. Competitive sport (e.g. rugby, basketball, badminton)
2. Physical recreation (non-competitive activities which are usually conducted on an informal basis, e.g. rambling, cycling, sailing)
3. Aesthetic activities (e.g. movement and dance)

4. Conditioning activities (those engaged in primarily for health and fitness benefits, e.g. aerobics, weight training, exercise to music).

Sport is gender-, age- and ability-inclusive, ranging from young children to the retired and from the elite to the disabled. It can be varied in intensity from highly competitive to instructional and from team sports to wilderness activities. Sports ministry takes this broad base and, by means of varied activities, seeks to serve the purposes of God as he builds his church through the redeeming death of his Son. It provides stimulation to those wishing to use their physical talent for God's glory and the extension of his Kingdom, as well as a motivation towards personal witnessing in the sports arena. Out of this mix may come the missionary, the sports minister, the lay leader and the effective witness for Jesus Christ.

Muscular Christianity

This was a term birthed in the nineteenth century that sought to combine vigour and robustness with a strong commitment to living the Christian life with every sinew and fibre. The improvement of many aspects of society, as well as the production of a vibrant church, were seen to be immediate spin-offs from this movement that gathered pace on both sides of the Atlantic. It was, however, in the writings of two English authors, Charles Kingsley and Thomas Hughes, that the concept was first born. Hughes, in particular, though probably influenced by Kingsley, used strong muscular Christian ideas in his internationally well-known books, *Tom Brown's Schooldays* and *Tom Brown in Oxford*, emphasizing regularly the powerful combination in one person, Tom Brown, of manliness, morality and spirituality. Kingsley drove home the point in 1874 with the publication of *Health and Education*. In it, he listed the many virtues that can come from the playing of games and which no book could teach. His list included daring, endurance, honour, fairness, self-control and commending the success of others. Little did Kingsley know that within a decade a sporting English family would serve to illustrate many of his findings.

The Cricketing Studds

The Studd family earned their place in the Muscular Christian movement when all three of Edward Studd's sons became Christians and captains of cricket during their time at Cambridge University. Charles (C.T.), in his short time in the England team, was a stunning all rounder of the Ian Botham mould, at a time when English cricket ruled the world. He came back from a Test series in Australia in 1885 only to find his brother George (G.B.) seriously ill. For Charles at that time the words of 1 Timothy 4:8 seemed particularly significant:

> For physical training is of some value, but godliness has value for all things, holding promise for both the present life and the life to come.

His brother's illness put life into perspective and within a short period of time C.T. had retired from international cricket, much to the consternation of both selectors and supporters alike. Instead, he prepared himself to go as a member of the 'Cambridge Seven' to China on missionary duty. C.T. had become, in a matter of a few years, the first Muscular Christian to gain national and international recognition as both an evangelical Christian and an outstanding sportsman. One is tempted to feel disappointed at C.T.'s removal from the international cricketing stage, knowing the influence his faith could have brought to bear. However, as the story unfolds, it is worth noting that the verse from 1 Timothy says 'some value' not 'no value' and Charles was at pains to write home to his brothers, evoking them to both enjoy their sport and give thanks to Jesus for their giftings. Indeed, C.T. himself was able to join a cricket tour to India in 1904 where he had gone on missionary service. The tour enabled him to 'play for the glory of God' and make use of the opportunities to meet with soldiers in different parts of the subcontinent and share his faith. His ability and fame meant that large crowds were always keen to hear about his life story and many responded to the call of salvation.

The Studds in the USA

The link between the Studd family and the USA was always a strong one, from the time of Edward Studd's conversion as a result of the D.L. Moody campaigns. When Charles dispersed his personal fortune prior to his departure for China, a good portion of this went to Moody for evangelical purposes, and Kyneston Studd (J.E.K.) responded to Moody's invitation to tour American colleges and talk about his sport and his faith. Indeed, most of the 'Cambridge Seven' became Christians through the influence and preaching of Moody who saw the value of reaching the sporting subculture by being involved in all that went on there. Such was his competitiveness, that any cricket game he played in usually included one of the Studd boys in his team so that the chances of victory were measurably improved.

The many spin-offs to this partnership between the Studds and Moody helped forge even stronger ties between evangelical Christianity and sport. Out of this engagement came the founding of the Student Volunteer Movement (SVM) and the greater emphasis in the YMCA movement on the role of sport for reaching the youth of America. It had, indeed, been a significant day in 1877 when Edward Studd, a wealthy English tea planter, trusted Christ at one of Moody's revival campaigns. Both men, in their own right, became history makers in the embryonic days of sports ministry in England and America.

The Birth of Church Sports Ministry

It was in the twentieth century when the modern movement of sports ministry really got underway. A political leader in Taiwan, after the Second World War, contacted a Christian basketball group in the USA and invited them over to coach their sport and share their faith. Shortly after this, in 1954, the organization Fellowship of Christian Athletes (FCA) was birthed, starting initially as an American camp ministry for young people. Other sports ministries followed, in particular what is now the largest international sports ministry, Athletes in Action (AIA). The emphasis in these early days was plainly with high profile athletes, students on university campuses and amongst the youth. It was only in the second half of the century that the public's consuming interest in sport led to the realization that sports ministry, in the context of the local church, was a vast untapped field. As with their ministry to high profile athletes it was the organizations in the USA that also led the way in this new phenomenon.

The Local Church – God's 'A' Plan

God's plan for man's salvation in Christ has not deviated since the first century, when a mixed bunch of individuals waited in Jerusalem for the promise that would rock the world – the coming of the Holy Spirit. The fellowship of believers, known later as the local church, became heaven's mechanism for change and the medium through which God proclaims his free gift of eternal life through faith in his son Jesus. Such a local church needs to be a solid and effective part of its community, role modelling the Kingdom of God to a world that is perishing in its own selfishness. It needs to adapt to cultural changes and constantly have an eye on where people are to be found and what their changing needs are. In a sentence, the local church is ready-made for sports evangelism.

In a sentence, the local church is ready-made for sports evangelism

Growth in the UK

In 1993, Christians in Sport invited Rodger Oswald of Church Sports International (CSI) to leave the Golden State of California for a short while in order to visit the UK with the express purpose of stimulating the organization into considering the development of a new department, Church Sport and Recreation Ministry. Christians in Sport wanted to be an active resource to churches already involved in sports ministry as well as those wanting to know how they could start.

Edward Studd and D.L. Moody would have been proud of the continuation of the plan they had set in motion a century or so earlier.

Rodger toured the major cities as well as being the keynote speaker at Christians in Sport's national conference in Shropshire. The author found himself at that conference as a volunteer worker with Christians in Sport but also masquerading as a deputy headmaster from a Yorkshire comprehensive school. Through God's leading and Rodger's ministry that weekend, a series of events were set in motion. Christians in Sport advertised the post of national co-ordinator for church sports ministry to which I successfully applied.

Coming out of teaching after thirty years was a big decision, especially since Garforth Community College, where I had taught for the previous sixteen years, was a flagship for the Leeds Authority in so many ways. I had spent many occasions at the Civic Hall in Leeds listening to parents, whose children were on an extensive waiting list, giving their reasons why they were anxious for their child to be awarded a place at GCC. For most of my time at Garforth, the school had been piloted by Lawrie Lowton who had gained an OBE for his exceptional service to Education in Leeds. Lawrie's challenging Christian faith and leadership made working at the College a real privilege and, being part of the management team, a real challenge. As one whose advice I value above all others, his support for our new venture was both encouraging and unwavering. He continues to be a strong supporter of the work I do and is the Chairman of Trustees for Higher Sports, the Christian sports charity I lead.

Go Onto the World's Field

The church of Jesus Christ has been issued with a clear commission from its founder. It is to 'preach the good news to all creation' (Mark 16:15) at any and every opportunity, wherever people are gathered. Jesus had role modelled this principle before crowds in the synagogue, at weddings, funerals and on the hillsides of Galilee.

In an age when people gather in their thousands at leisure clubs, stadiums, aerobics studios, fun runs and golf clubs, it becomes vital for those Christians found naturally in these areas to live the Christian life and tell their story to their friends.

We are commanded further to proclaim 'forgiveness of sins' (Luke 24:47). In the intense cauldron of sport, how readily self-interest and self-importance take centre stage with little thought given to the plight or otherwise of one's opponent. The situation can easily become gladiatorial rather than attaining the true meaning of competition which is 'to strive together' or, to use the words of the Olympic ideal, 'it's not the winning it's the taking part' (Baron Pierre de Coubertin). The sporting Christian demonstrates true sportsmanship when he or she is able to role model the truth of Ephesians 4:32 – 'Be kind and compassionate to one another, forgiving each other, just as in Christ God forgave you.' What a privilege to demonstrate God's gift of forgiveness in the arena of sport. Those of you who have had some intense situations in this arena will know what I mean when I describe it as a gift, heaven-sent.

Another vital aspect of God's command to the church is to 'make disciples' (Matthew 28:19). The very nature of sport with its strong relational connotation offers enormous potential as a Christ-centred environment. There is a potential to teach, train and transmit on a regular and ongoing basis. No finer example is that of Jason Robinson, the former rugby international who has represented his country at both codes, rugby union and rugby league. The arrival of Va'aiga Tuigamala, the Western Samoan All Black, at Jason's club,

Wigan, in the middle of the 1990s served to change this young man's life to the very core. His interview with *The Times* on 1 November 1999 revealed the significance of this burgeoning relationship:

> I saw this man who played the same game as me but didn't need all the going out and drinking. He was at peace with himself. There was something there that I wanted, so I talked to him about it and he explained his faith. I used to be one of the lads and was down at the pub all the time. I've not been in a pub drinking for four years. There's more to life than sitting in a smelly pub.

As 'Inga' Tuigamala first witnessed to Jason and then discipled him, a mature and purposeful Christian life began to develop in this outstanding rugby player. Following Inga's example, Jason joined a church and started combing through his Bible. He soon started helping to improve the lives of the socially deprived and began to play all his games with wrist bands marked with a cross. The latter has no superstitious link but, rather, recommends and glorifies his Saviour in the arena where he first met him. Who better to disciple in the world of sport than the one who is involved in the world of sport. As Jason was taught and trained by his good friend Inga, he was then confident to communicate his own personal faith in Christ at any and every opportunity as regular media reports indicate. There can be no greater privilege for the Christian sportsman than to lead a teammate to Christ and then play a significant part in his Christian growth.

The Sporting Christian

When Jesus was born into an ordinary family and first visited by shepherds, it was God's way of saying that 'no go' areas in the providence of heaven don't exist. The prayer of Jesus in John 17:18 acknowledges this very truth and then builds on it with the words 'I have sent them into the world'. That divine mystery which enabled God to visit us in human form is particularly significant in the sporting world. In the same way that God communicates with man through his Son's humanity, so the sporting Christian enters that vast subculture of sport with the same life-changing message. The prophet Ezekiel was given clear instructions to take God's words to a people who spoke the same language and had a similar understanding (Ezekiel 3:4–6). The language of sport is arguably the most unifying bond on the face of this earth.

The language of sport is arguably the most unifying bond on the face of this earth

Unfortunately, the church equates mission with foreign lands and ministry in a different culture. Whilst not denying this sending procedure, it seems only too obvious that sharing the gospel with whom you have most in common and where you are most at home has to be significant in the economy of God. Instead of the local church bemoaning the fact that one of their members has his priorities wrong because he prefers rugby practice to the midweek Bible study, they would do well to bring the rugby club into the parameters of their mission outreach strategy. This would put a whole new emphasis on their colleague's gifting in the world of rugby. He now becomes a branch of Christ's church in the rugby club and would no doubt be encouraged by the midweek group praying for his opportunities to share with teammates the difference Jesus can make in their lives. Members of the church turning up to watch games and relate to the rugby club fraternity would equally serve to expand the influence of God's Kingdom in that particular community.

It is unfortunate that the common conception of sports ministry is that of well-known athletes drawing a crowd to a church function, sports dinner or crusade. The erroneous belief is that they should be 'sent' around the country advancing the gospel by their fame and popularity. It is to the credit of the Christians in Sport organization that they refuse to abuse their strong relationships with high profile athletes by behaving in such a way. They believe their God-given role to be one of support for the athlete in the very area where their gifting and anointing have placed them, amongst their teammates and opponents. Here is the 'sent' area, their 'Jerusalem, Judaea, Samaria and the ends of the earth' (Acts 1:8).

The Church Team

For many years now, Rodger Oswald, of Church Sports International, has emphasized that a travelling sports team should be the natural outgrowth of a sports ministry or a discipleship training programme that has taken time to train the athlete as well as develop his ministry gifts. Rodger believes this can begin with such a team playing in a church league and including in their training programme Bible study sessions that explore the individual's standing in Christ and how they can use their talents to serve him. The next step may be to join a secular league with the high priority of sharing their faith through competition in a more

hostile environment. Bible studies under these circumstances would include such topics as how to give your testimony, share the gospel in a sports setting and develop
relationships. Coming under scrutiny would be the progress
made in 'walking the walk' on the field of play as well as
'talking the talk'. It would not be a quantum leap from this
situation for the team to then begin to visit detention centres
and prisons to both play and share their faith with the
inmates. The team may finally plan an overseas venture with
the express purpose of supporting and encouraging the local
church to reach out beyond its community through the
medium of sport. Some years ago, whilst in California, I met
with Jim Urbanovich, the Sports Pastor at Emmanuel
Church, Los Angeles. As well as running a very full and pro-
ductive sport and recreation programme, Jim had taken the
church's men's basketball team on a ten-day tour in Brazil.
Over that period, they had played in front of 25,000 people,
sharing their testimonies during the half-time intervals.
Many of the spectators became Christians and many others
were put in contact with the local churches.

Rodger Oswald concludes in his philosophy of sending
such teams '. . . the commitment of Church Sports
International is to recruit and participate in the training and
equipping of athletes so that they have a positive influence
on the mission field they visit, that the life of the athlete is
forever changed because of the training and that their experience and resultant joy infects the entire church as they
share and stimulate on their return'.

Power in the Arena

To be a witness in the world of sport and recreation, whether
at 'home' or 'away' (Acts 1:8) is part of the Christian's job

description. It goes with the territory and is not confined to personality or occasion. With the present explosion of interest in both the leisure industry and international sporting competitions, there is a harvest field all ready for workers to enter with their sleeves rolled up. Gone are the days when the evangelist could hit town and speak to a full tent in the evening. Nowadays, the technological pace of life provides too many evening distractions for those who might have made their way to the tent crusade. However, there is no shortage of large crowds. It is just that they are now found on playing fields or inside sporting arenas. If Jesus commissioned his disciples to go into all the world, then we don't need a chapter and verse to convince us that a large part of that world is involved in sport and recreation, whether by interest or participation. The further evidence from Scripture is that Jesus never commissions except he empowers at the same time. It was for this reason that his earthly 'team' were commanded to wait in Jerusalem for the power of the Holy Spirit and then to go and be witnesses both at home and abroad.

To be a witness in the world of sport and recreation, whether at 'home' or 'away' (Acts 1:8) is part of the Christian's job description

Receiving the Call to Sports Ministry

There can be no more exciting occasion in an athlete's life than to be 'called up' to compete for his or her country. I remember a young man I taught, Chris Silverwood, getting excited when he was selected to play for the School Under 12 cricket team. One can only imagine how he felt a few years later when he was also 'called up' in turn by the England Under 19 side, the Yorkshire County Championship team and finally, the full England Test XI.

To fulfil God's command is to respond to a heavenly 'call up' which can take on three forms. Firstly, the *general* call is the one received by all who decide to follow Christ and is encapsulated in the call that came to the disciples to become 'fishers of men' in Matthew 4:19. This call is not an optional extra or a special gifting. Rather it goes with the job description and should be the Christian's life-long mission. The rugby player becomes a 'fisher' of rugby players and the golfer a 'fisher' of golfers. Wherever God places us is the place where we seek to impact the Kingdom of God and make a difference. The sports world is a huge harvest field and as needy as most.

To fulfil God's command is to respond to a heavenly 'call up'

Secondly, Paul advises us in his letter to the church at Corinth, (2 Corinthians 5:17–20) that we are not only fishers but also 'ambassadors'. It is a *personal* call to represent God and serve him in a foreign land. The lone Christian in the netball team should not bemoan the fact that she is the only one there but rather rejoice in the privilege of being God's ambassador in the side. Without her there would be no fragrance of Christ in that arena. When you also consider that an ambassador comes with the full protection of their Sovereign, then this is certainly a 'call up' to take seriously.

Finally, there is the *special* call of God on the Christian athlete. This is the call to use your gifting, talents and positioning to advance the cause of Christ in the lives of those you are able to influence by your lifestyle and conversation. Paul's instruction to Archippus in Colossians 4:17 was very much along these lines when he told him to 'complete the work' that he had 'received in the Lord'.

Some of you who read this book might feel that your ministry is to be in the world of sport and that this is your 'special' calling. If so, then it is a call that needs to be understood also by the church and its leadership so that the individual can be recognized as the church's arm into the sporting world. Indeed, when the Apostle Paul recognized certain gifts in people he saw to it that they were 'set aside' for the work and equipped for their ministry. In the same way, the Christian athlete should seek to fulfil all that God has invested in him. It may be as a national or international figure, an influential coach, a keen local team player, a physical education teacher or a youth leader with a sporting passion. In all cases, the significance of this position in the world of sport must not be underestimated.

The Church's Response

The individual fulfils the command of God by responding to the call of God but how does the church similarly respond? In a hostile world it needs to be constantly reaching upward, inward and outward in order to be the very best that God intended.

In response to those well-known words recorded in the Westminster catechism summarizing man's chief end – 'to love God and enjoy him forever' – the church reaches upward in worship. Before gazing inward and outward the focus must always be upward towards the Creator who holds all things together by his power and might. In upward gazing and experiencing the sheer enjoyment of God for who he is – a state that can be as significant on the sports field as in the church pew – the Christian is then stimulated to grow in faith and reach inward. The Apostle Paul provokes his fellow worker, Timothy, to be 'equipped for every good work' (2 Timothy 3:17) by allowing the Word of God to determine his inward journey by being embedded in every aspect of his life.

However, if the church were to spend all its time concentrating on the upward and inward side of its necessary development, then the Great Commission given by Jesus to his disciples on the ascension mount would be invalidated. He departed having invested his life-blood into his church, knowing that if the world was to 'call on the one they have not believed in' (Romans 10:14) then the outward activity of believers was paramount. After saying that preaching needs to be commissioned by God, Paul then quotes Isaiah 52:7: 'How beautiful . . . are the feet of those who bring good news'. The sporting world will only hear of the one they have not believed in as the 'beautiful feet' of fellow sportsmen and women take this life-changing message into their subculture.

Just Do It

The Athenians in the ancient world were determined that Nike, the goddess of victory, would remain in their city temple and so they clipped her wings to ensure her continual presence and, with it, all future victories. The Christian requires no such superstitious idol and is encouraged by Paul's rallying call to the church in Rome when he told them they were 'more than conquerors through him who loved us' (Romans 8:37).

Within the context of the local church, God has determined that his work will be accomplished. If the church is to employ sport and recreation as part of its game-plan then certain biblical principles must be central to the work.

Firstly, the principle of divine diversity opens up the way for man to use his kaleidoscopic gifting in the sporting world in order to proclaim the good news of Jesus Christ. The nature and character of God rejoices in the diversity yet oneness of the Trinity and, in the person of Jesus, we see a referral to many titles and descriptions. He is the Lamb of God, the Light of the World, the Way, the Truth, the Life, the Door, the Vine, etc. The Word of God in creation and God's diverse ministry in the lives of Abraham, Moses, Joseph, David, Peter, Paul and many more, are all indications that we are to use the gifts, calling and positioning that God has bestowed upon us.

Paul invokes the Christians in Galatia not to be burdened by the yoke of slavery because it is Christ who has set them free (Galatians 5:1). By the same token, those of us who are called to sports ministry are free from man-made conventions and traditions. This same principle of liberty is reinforced by Paul in his writings to the church at Corinth but with a different twist. Although he is free, he is prepared to make himself a slave to everyone in order to win as many as possible for God's Kingdom. He is ready to go into any area and any subculture so that he can openly proclaim that he has become 'all things to all men so that by all possible means I might save some' (1 Corinthians 9:22). What a clarion call here for sport and recreation ministry – to take the gospel into the frenetic and intense cauldron of physical activity and seek to live the life that Christ has set us free to enjoy. No wonder that later in the same chapter of 1 Corinthians 9 Paul remarks 'Everyone who competes in the games goes into strict training . . . we do it to get a crown that will last for ever' (verse 25). What a privilege, what a calling!

Competition

The principle of preparing someone for a competitive world can be easily ignored, if not dismissed, by the church. Yet in the early chapters of Genesis we see the competitive strands of creation (Genesis 1:28) and then the full force of sin and its consequences (Genesis 3:15,17,19). Centuries later, Peter, writing from Rome (1 Peter 5:8), is mindful of the same forces to be combated when he encouraged his readers to 'Be self-controlled and alert. Your enemy the devil prowls around like a roaring lion looking for someone to devour.' Paul also reminds the church at Ephesus that 'our struggle is not against flesh and blood, but against the rulers, against the authorities, against the powers of this dark world and against the spiritual forces of evil in the heavenly realms' (Ephesians 6:12). Now there's a competition to be prepared for!

As with many things, the world has turned 'competition' into something quite different from the original intention. Greg Linville believes that many competitors are caught up in and believe in the 'win at all costs' philosophy of sports. They would follow the motto of the late Vince Lombardi, legendary American gridiron football coach – 'winning isn't everything, it's the only thing'.

The ultimate accomplishment for many is winning and this is achieved by 'blowing away' your opponent who is often seen consequentially as useless and inept. Such a position would have no place in a sports ministry programme and would be the very antithesis of the Christian philosophy to competition. However, it does serve to put grist in the mill of those who would wish to dispose of all competition. I remember in the 1970s dealing with a number of head teachers who had cancelled all competitive fixtures with other schools and replaced them with internal friendly activities where there were no winners or losers. To my mind, these head teachers were failing in their responsibilities to their charges in a big way. The youngsters were at a stage in their lives when they needed positive leadership and guidance on how to cope with and react to opponents in the heat of competition. They were entering a world where there would be plenty of influential people only too ready to teach them 'Lombardi rules' and they needed the right kind of role models to see them through. You see, competition is not unlike money in that it is a neutral force. Whether it becomes a force for good or evil depends on the way athletes react in the heat of it. However, to remove it from the circle of activity would handicap spiritual development rather than advance it. The final thought on this controversial subject goes to Greg Linville again with his proposal that Christian athletes must emulate Jesus Christ in everything they do, including their whole attitude to competition. He recommends they take on the mantle of 'Christmanship' rather than 'the humanistically based ethic of sportsmanship and the pragmatically based ethic of gamesmanship'. Christmanship is to compete in the image of Christ in the way you connect with teammates, opponents, officials and coaches. It involves competing with zeal and unmatched enthusiasm, whilst honouring your opponent as you play your very best. I need an opponent in order to hone and improve the skills that God has endowed me with. If my opponent is on top form then I seek to raise my standards accordingly so that we both profit from this God-given principle. Equally, if I have the edge in the game I would hope to bring the best out of him as we compete together.

Race of Life

The Bible makes no specific reference to the relevance or otherwise of sports ministry but speaks volumes in its silence. If 'all Scripture' is there 'for teaching, rebuking, correcting and training in righteousness' (2 Timothy 3:16) then it seems more than unusual that there are no pronouncements against athletic activities if they are for worldly use only. On the contrary, the Apostle Paul's writings are studded with reference after reference to athletic analogies that were used to encourage and bolster the many Christian communities in Asia Minor and Rome. Paul told Timothy he was 'being poured out like a drink offering' (2 Timothy 4:6) in the way the athlete poured out his gifts of wine and food as an offering to the gods before competing, and that he had 'finished the race' (2 Timothy 4:7). The crown awaiting the athlete in the stadium was so often compared to God's 'crown of righteousness' awarded 'on that day' (2 Timothy 4:8) and he finally exhorted the believers at Philippi to 'press on towards the goal to win the prize' (Philippians 3:14).

Paul's writings are studded with reference after reference to athletic analogies

In the book of Hebrews, the spiritual athlete is encouraged to 'run with perseverance' the race of life and 'throw off everything that hinders' (12:1), the latter a reference to the athlete abandoning the weights normally carried in the hands when running. The 'great cloud of witnesses' that surround this event at the end of life's race is graphically enacted every four years when millions of people around the world witness the reception given to the marathon runners in the Olympic Games as they finish the course.

One of the most moving moments for me from the 2000 Sydney Olympics was when one of the British marathon runners picked up an injury within minutes of the start but completed the course in pain and over one hour behind the last runner. On being interviewed, he gave his reasons for completing the course as pride in his country, gratitude for those who had helped him qualify for the Olympics, and a determination not to give up after four years of preparation. He had been given as tumultuous a reception in the stadium as the one received by the gold medal winner. What a promise there is for the spiritual athlete when he enters that great heavenly stadium and first catches sight of Jesus waiting for him at the finishing tape. A race completed thanks to the firm footings in that very same Son of God and a life that has been aimed to go 'beyond the gold'.

2

PREPARING THE BID

Opportunities for success in this world are as great as we have the imagination to dream them

John Maxwell

Sports Ministry is Biblical!

It started well

To understand the role of sport in God's creative plan we need to take a look at the book of Genesis. Here we find an affirmation of God's desire that we go out and enjoy the world he has created for us. If we are to seek to image God in all that we do, then our major concentration must be in the two areas of creativity and relationships.

In the first chapter of Genesis, we see what was, in effect, God's playground. God's excitement and enjoyment of his creation is captured by the constant reference to the phrase 'it was good' (verses 10, 12, 18, 21 and 25). After the creation was complete with the formation of man, the text moves up a gear with the words 'it was very good' (verse 31).

God made us last, with the proviso that we should worship him first

God made us last, with the proviso that we should worship him first. We are encouraged to take hold of creation on his behalf and enhance it. The abilities needed to participate in sport – hand/eye co-ordination, quick feet, spatial awareness, natural spring, etc. – are inherent in humankind and God is delighted when we honour him by the way we play it and the attitude we show in doing so. Jesus expressed it another way when he said, 'I have come that they may have life, and have it to the full' (John 10:10).

It is interesting to note that the verbs used in Genesis 2:15 for 'to work' and 'to take care of' are the same verbs that are used later in the Old Testament to indicate the priests' acts of worship in the tabernacle and the temple. God wants us to see that what we do throughout the week is simply a different form of worship from that which happens on the Sabbath. For those of us excited by the world of sport then that means offering our bodies 'as living sacrifices' (Romans 12:1) in worship to God by the way we fulfil the gifting he has given us in this area.

The second major area to consider as we look at Genesis is that of relationships. Our God is in community and has always had companionship. In Genesis 1:26 we see this clearly presented with the record 'let us make man in our image'. As those in God's image we are made to live in community and reflect God in the way we work together. In sporting terms this means we need to have someone to play with in order to make the game worthwhile. There is a limit to the number of times you can keep hitting a ball against the wall. It is important to be stretched and challenged by teammates and opponents.

Now here is the rub. If it is valid for us to invest huge chunks of our time in sport, then we must work out whether this is of God. If we are able to love our opponents as ourselves, as God would want us to do, then this is an area where we can glorify

God and grow in his presence. To 'give thanks to God' in all that we do (Colossians 3:17) and at the same time honour our opponents means that we can push out the boundaries of our own giftings and maximize our ability to serve God. It will then be possible to become stronger players in every sense: more committed to excellence and with a desire to be pushed to the highest level. We will quickly learn that being in God's team on the sports field means that winning is not enough. What is enough is to have gone out and played for God. He is in the fullest sense 'the audience of One'.

Athletes in the New Testament

The Apostle Paul is noted for his many athletic references in his epistles. He was fully aware of the interests people had in the culture of the day and he constantly drew parallels and made comparisons between the challenges of both the physical and the spiritual life. In this respect, he was following the example of Jesus, whose parabolic ministry gave high profile to shepherds and farmers. He wanted to make it as easy as possible for every one of his listeners to make the transfer from the principles of this world to the principles of the Kingdom of God. As Jesus moved among men and women in the places of their own security, he lived an incarnational life not an informational one. He was in their midst as 'Immanuel', God with them, who was able to change their lives and their circumstances for the better. He was the original 'fresh expression' of God in a world that found itself under the heaviness of religious tradition.

The Apostle Paul picks up the same theme in his letter to the Corinthian Church and in the ninth chapter of his first letter. He has credibility for preaching the gospel of Jesus Christ because he has made himself utterly available to the people as their servant in order to win them for his Saviour (verse 19). He does what they are doing and, unless it is sinful, goes where they are going. In what has become a classic verse for sports ministry of any kind he says that 'I have become all things to all men so that by all possible means I might save some' (verse 22). He is constantly seeking to bring heaven down into as many circumstances and situations as he can manufacture. A fine role model for the budding sports minister!

When Paul continued to use such words as 'race', 'the games' and 'strict training' in verses 24 and 25, he was aware of the large people group that adopted this phraseology as part of their lifestyle. He wanted to become an insider so that he would have the credibility to share the life-changing news of Christ's death and resurrection. D.L. Moody summed it up succinctly when he said, 'Of a hundred people searching for Jesus Christ, one will read the Bible and ninety-nine will read the Christians.'

Poor Fit?

Those not convinced about the relevance of sport and recreation ministry in the local church would believe there to be a dichotomy between the selfishness of professional sport and the commands of Jesus to esteem others better than themselves. Indeed, some church pronouncements in the past have ventured to describe sport as sinful although, thankfully, those days seem to be getting more distant.

We find no reference to the word 'secular' in the Scriptures

The whole area of dualism is unbiblical. We find no reference to the word 'secular' in the Scriptures but many exhortations to 'give thanks in everything'. The life God intends us to live is like a seamless robe and there should be no sacred/secular divide. We glorify God by our actions in the aerobics class or on the games field as much as we do in worship at the Sunday morning service. The former activities have us reaching outward to people, whilst the latter has us reaching upward to God. Both complement the teaching and edification role within the church where the inward reaching for growth is the final piece of the jigsaw that equips the body of Christ to 'go and make disciples' (Matthew 28:19).

Modern example

There is no finer example of a Christian athlete than that of Eric Liddell in the last century. Seeing himself as a steward of his body and its capabilities, he was also aware of the body's role as a temple for the Holy Spirit. With this in mind, he sought to express his love and commitment to God through the way he ran his races and played the game of rugby. Julian Wilson seeks to explain the secret of Liddell's success on the track in his book *Complete Surrender*, a biography of the athlete:

> To glorify God by striving for perfection without compromise. That is not to say that Liddell's creed was to win at all costs. Running exhilarated him and he loved to win, to prove he was the best in his event, but he never sought personal glory nor revelled in his exceptional athletic ability. Magnanimous in defeat he had no lust for victory. When a friend asked him whether he ever prayed that he would win a race Liddell replied characteristically, 'No, I have never prayed that I would win a race. I have, of course, prayed about the athletic meeting that in this too, God might be glorified.'

Sports Ministry is Relevant!

Tony Ladd, co-author of the book *Muscular Christianity* with James A. Mathisen, notes the re-emergence of the muscular Christianity movement towards the end of the twentieth century but issues a grave warning:

> As we enter a new millennium, Christians are operating outside the culture they are trying to transform.

For society to be transformed by the Word of God it has to be first of all penetrated by the people of God. Sport, like music, is a universal language that transcends barriers of creed, class and culture. It allows the Christian sportsman and woman to role model the gospel in any and every situation. Doors open all over the world to the Christian sportsman in countries that would be barred to the Christian missionary. The sports ambassador role is a privileged one which must be used wisely.

Sport, like music, is a universal language that transcends barriers of creed, class and culture

A colleague of mine, Carl Dambman, works for Athletes in Action in Moscow and was taking wrestling teams into Russia long before the Communist regime fell in the early 1990s. He was welcomed into the country because of his sporting ability and love for the Russian people. He was then able to use his God-given talent to witness to his wrestling opponents. Carl wrestled internationally in the super heavyweight class for the USA and was national champion, Pan American champion and took the bronze medal in the 1979 Madrid World Championships. He has a pretty impressive testimony and would certainly have his opponents' attention once his considerable weight was upon them! His team would also work with the underground church during their tours and, as well as worshipping and encouraging the Russian Christians, they would regularly supply them with literature and Bibles. Carl works with much more freedom these days from the very heart of Moscow but, in those days, his wrestling 'ticket' was the only way he could get into the country and share Jesus. His email signature 'in his grip' certainly comes to life once you have met him!

A similar situation occurs in the Middle East where a Christian Arabic church has a strong sports ministry team of young people. As well as giving much time to the coaching of Muslim youngsters in their own country, the church sends small teams into countries like Iran, Iraq, Saudi Arabia, Syria, etc. Wonderful stories abound of all the blessings that have flowed out of these ventures.

Young people

In the late 1970s, Judith and I, together with another couple, were pioneering a church plant in Wetherby, West Yorkshire. We were due to hold our first service and were anxious to start a Sunday club at the same time for children and young people. We had three young boys, and our friends David and Margaret had three young girls. The Friday evening before the first service saw the ten of us occupying a grassy area near to the church premises and close to where the local youngsters gathered. A loud and frenetic game of rounders-cum-softball caught nearby interest and before long we had a good number of the local children involved in the game.

Refreshments and introductions concluded a very happy evening and when invitations were given for Sunday Club a positive response was received. Many years later, a solid group from this initial 'sports' outreach was still part of the ongoing youth work.

I am convinced that the sports evangelist could turn up anywhere in the world with ball under arm and have a group to share the gospel with inside an hour. Sport itself gives a unity to any situation and accelerates friendship and bonding by its very rules. On a recent visit to Turkey, I was invited to join some local young men playing volleyball. High fives replaced language communication and an invitation to play again a few days later confirmed the effectiveness and cultural relevance of sports ministry. How often has the street evangelist been approached by the local people and asked to take up his position and do it all again? In a country like Turkey, the most unreached nation for Christ in the world – only 3,000 believers in a nation of 65 million – I'm convinced that sport and recreation ministry would be the most effective conduit for the gospel. There is a quick binding commonality in sport that is quite unique to other areas where people gather.

Friends

Derek, like me, was in his 'middle years', but unlike me had represented England Youth at football and played as a professional with West Bromwich Albion and other league clubs. He was the father of one of my pupils at school, and his wife Jenny was a faithful supporter of the parent teachers' group I organized. After they had accepted an invitation to come to our home for a Christmas celebration evening, Derek agreed to join me on a men's challenge weekend at an outdoor centre in the Yorkshire Dales.

Derek's enthusiasm for recreational comradeship was a real joy to observe but it got even more exciting when he became a Christian before the weekend was out. Further weekends of the same ilk, sports outreach dinners and church five-a-side competitions, all contributed to Derek growing as a Christian and joining our house fellowship group with Jenny. The non-threatening nature of the sporting environments had been largely responsible for Derek's entry into the Kingdom of God.

Students

One of our sons, Ben, with a small group of Christian sporting friends at university, organized a sports outreach meal for all their teammates in the university squads. Operating within the subculture of university sport, they were up front with their Christian faith and particularly encouraged when around 100 of their friends turned up from rugby and hockey teams, gymnastic classes and the canoe club. They had quickly realized that you had to earn the right to share the good news of Jesus by meeting folk where they were and penetrating the culture. It was an additional encouragement when a number from the dinner signed up to join discussions on investigating the Christian faith. The whole evening was a fine example of sports ministry being culturally relevant and reaching a group otherwise untouched on university campus. A local church had helped with the financing of the meal and provided a strong link for the follow-up meetings.

Family

Sports ministry helps to assimilate people into the life of the church. We were privileged a few years ago to be present at the start of a children's football (soccer) programme organized by a church in Los Gatos, California. All morning and well into the afternoon children from 6–12 years of age turned up in droves to learn skills, play games and receive biblical teaching. There were facilities and hot snacks for parents while they waited and many of them watched and listened in to the devotional time at the end of each session. The church's director of sport told us that he had seen many families brought to faith in Christ by initially signing up their 6-year-old for the soccer programme. Such vibrant mornings of activity enable the local church to serve and witness to the community in a way that it can never do through its more traditional approaches. In my opinion, this type of programme is a must for any church wanting to be at the cutting edge in their community. Through godly care, attention and time given to the young, the impact on the rest of the family can be immense.

Discipleship

A cultural strategy within sport and recreation ministry is the platform it creates for discipleship. The relationships naturally formed within a sporting context provide the ideal area for the mature believer to disciple the new Christian. As well as building up their friendship level, time can also be carved out for Bible study, prayer and sharing their faith with others. Instruction and accountability take place in the very area where the disciple and the discipler long to be and spend the majority of their time.

When Graham Daniels, the General Director of Christians in Sport, was playing professional soccer with Cambridge United, he found his position under threat from a new signing, Alan Comfort. Graham's positive attitude to Alan's signing, and a concerted effort to help assimilate him into the club and its playing strategies, impressed the new recruit and a deep friendship ensued. Graham shared his Christian faith openly with Alan and before long Alan became a Christian. The two men spent much time in each other's company and grew in their Christian lives as disciple and discipler. Alan later signed for Middlesborough and after turning over his knee in a match against Newcastle United he had to take early retirement from the game. He is now an Anglican minister and amongst his many duties he has helped to disciple young men and women from the Christians in Sport Academy and so continues the many discipleship opportunities that are possible within the arena of sport.

Diversity

Sports ministry has an ability to reach where other ministries can never hope to go. As a cultural phenomenon, it provides unique access to people. I remember watching the close of the US Masters Golf Competition in Augusta on Easter Sunday 1993 when Bernhard Langer was giving his victory speech. His first round of thanks was directed towards his Lord who had risen from the dead on this day and in whom Bernhard's hopes rested. The millions of interested, not to say fanatical, golfers around the world, were able to receive such a succinct life-giving message because of the golfing talent God had invested in Bernhard Langer. Such talent afforded the golfer tremendous access to and influence on many people around the world.

Sports ministry has an ability to reach where other ministries can never hope to go

There are few areas like sport where spiritual growth and maturity can be measured regularly. The intense cauldron of competition and performance quickly becomes a litmus test for the individual's progress in his walk with God. Making the correct observations and utterances at the players' Bible study holds little weight if this does not match up with attitude and behaviour on the field of play. The Christian character can sink without trace on these occasions, or stand out like a beacon in a selfish environment. There is no place for parade ground spirituality. It is time for the tin hat in the trenches as the battle is taken to the enemy. Winning with humility and losing with dignity become outward expressions of the changes that are taking place within.

There is no place for parade ground spirituality

The contribution of sport to physical, intellectual, social and spiritual growth is without question. It sharpens up these areas and enriches the life of the individual. The scripture reference in Luke 2:52 indicates the wholesome progress Jesus was making in these areas and how vital it is to progress on all fronts rather than let one or two dominate to the detriment of the others. To find a common denominator like sport that serves each area in equal measure can only be a unifying factor.

Finally, the gospel platform afforded to talented sportsmen and women is unique in its own right. For certain moments in their time-space continuum these athletes can be used by God as powerful role models in his Kingdom. The principle in force is the one revealed by Mordecai to Queen Esther in the book of Esther chapter 4 and verse 14, when he reminded her that she had risen to royal position 'for such a time as this'. So often in an athlete's life there are windows of opportunity for proclaiming the goodness and mercy of God. It was this same principle that prompted Bernhard Langer to make his famous Augusta speech on Easter Sunday in 1993.

Sports Ministry is Practical!

Any ministry may be biblically defensible and culturally relevant but the real testing point comes when it is put into practice. It is at this fulcrum point that sports ministry comes into its own.

It contributes positively to the mission of the church in reaching outward to a world without Christ. It takes the church out of its comfort zone and from within its own portals to the playing fields of life where needy people are to be found. The church does not have to attract a crowd since the crowd is already there, formed and vibrant. All it lacks is the life-saving message that only Jesus can bring. That's where Holy Spirit inspired practicality comes into its own.

It takes the church out of its comfort zone

Other ministries benefit

Other ministries in the church can profit enormously from the work of the sport and recreation department. Children from the holiday football clinic can be encouraged to join the Sunday club and Bible class. Ladies from the aerobics group can be invited to the weekly ladies fellowship gathering, whilst the speaker at the annual sports dinner can direct enquirers towards the group that is investigating

Christian belief over a period of weeks. The occasional Sunday Sports Service opens the way for believers to invite their friends and colleagues to a seeker-friendly proclamation of the gospel.

Fringe folk are drawn in

As well as drawing individuals in from the perimeter of church life, sport and recreation activities can also prevent others from drifting away. They provide regular activity and friendship for those who might otherwise be finding church too cerebral and in advance of the stage they are at on their spiritual journey. For many such individuals, a sports programme becomes the first step to re-creation in their own lives.

Ideal for new members

Bringing new members or new believers quickly into a place of ownership with the life of the church is an objective that most churches struggle with. Finding an entry level of service and recognizing gifts and talents does not figure high in most churches' mission statements. Sport and recreation are the ideal antidotes to this problem.

Leading an aerobics group or keep-fit class can bring the new member right into the centre of church life and relationships. The fact that another member of the group leads the devotional after 'warm down' does not detract from the valuable contribution made by the instructor who is key to the whole session. As the class develops, there may well come a time when the physical and spiritual content can be delivered by the same person. Success in one area is always a motivating force to press on into other areas where confidence is not immediately apparent. Recognition by the church of the new member's contribution to the life of the church through sport and recreation will do wonders for their desire to progress and play a positive role in the spiritual activities.

Community outreach works

Perhaps the greatest practical advantage of a sport and recreation ministry is that it enables the church to reach people who would otherwise remain unreached. Every community is interested in sport and recreation and is only too delighted when this is organized for them. They are happy to attend events that are run by enthusiastic people with care and attention.

I worked with a Cumbrian church on one occasion when a Christian farmer's field was turned into a sports arena for the Saturday afternoon. This little country church suddenly found itself host to all the village and took the opportunity to combine this event with a breakfast service the next day.

Leadership training opportunities

Leadership development within a church situation should be an integral part of any sports programme. The wide variety of activities can offer endless opportunities for such development at many different levels. As well as the director of the programme, there will be a need for others to take responsibility for different facets of the work and keep the progress within the aims and objectives of the ministry.

As sports ministry grows locally, nationally and internationally, there becomes a great need for men and women to respond to God's call. It may be as the sports pastor in a local church or as a key member of a parachurch ministry. It could equally be membership of a mission sports team working in urban areas or ministering abroad in countries that are not readily accessible to the gospel by orthodox means. As the leisure industry continues to grow and with it the universal passion for sport, this whitened harvest field cries out for those with a passion for Jesus and sport. What more natural place to be called of God than one where you can demonstrate the gifts he has given you and you can be in the midst of those whose real needs can only be met by Jesus.

Financial advantages

Despite all the many practical advantages of a sports ministry, there are those who would question the possible cost involved. This is a myth that needs nailing down because it couldn't be further from the truth. It is certainly helpful to have your own well-used facility. I say 'well-used' because many churches hire out their facilities to secular organizations rather than make them part of their own ministry. However, owning a facility is by no means necessary for an effectively run programme. In this day and age people are used to paying good money for their sports activities whether it be swimming, squash, five-a-side football, aerobics or a sports clinic. Sports centres, community centres and schools can be hired at competitive rates with the instruction and leadership taken by church members. It would be good use of the church's outreach fund to send its members on courses to train as coaches, aerobics instructors, community sports leaders, fell walkers and so on. The world cries out for organizations to offer such programmes and is even more impressed when they come with a real care for the community.

Church Growth Through Sport

Where churches have seriously adopted a sport and recreation ministry, a dramatic growth in the overall ministry has followed, with the lives of church members enriched and a commitment to Christ fostered. Four key reasons have contributed to this.

1. Mass appeal

In both the UK and USA the number of people discussing, reading about or participating in sport on a daily basis is in the 70 per cent plus category. For the church to have no designated strategy for reaching this huge people group is at best ignorance and at worst folly. When the Apostle Paul visited Athens for the first time, he determined that a new approach was called for and took the appropriate steps. In the case of the Athenians, it was their insatiable appetite for philosophy and religion that helped to fine-tune Paul's evangelistic goals, although he was also aware of their athletic prowess and the importance of the Athenian Games. His reference to the 'unknown god' in Acts 17:23 and his many athletic references in other letters clearly demonstrates this new approach to reach the Greeks for Christ. In similar fashion, the twenty-first-century church must equally learn to become all things to all men in order to save some.

For the church to have no designated strategy for reaching this huge people group is at best ignorance and at worst folly

2. *Men and young people*

Historically these are the two groups often missing from typical churches. Many churches tend to lose their young people when they transfer from primary to secondary school. A transition takes place that is neither understood nor catered for in the majority of churches. It is my supposition that sport could play a major role in shoring up this passage without major fall out. Otherwise the 11-year-old disappears from view and may not appear again until he is grown up and possibly has children of his own.

Many churches tend to lose their young people when they transfer from primary to secondary school

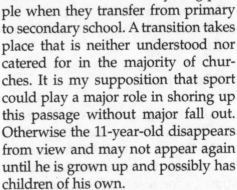

Adult men also seem to disappear into a black hole where church is concerned. This may be because of the church's insistence on verbal rather than physical talent as contributions. It can be argued that the youth and men have a hormonal need to be physically active which inevitably causes problems when trying to assimilate into a physically inactive church.

Before the sceptics amongst you accuse me of wanting to start the morning service with a work-out rather than an opening hymn, let me qualify the above comments. Sports ministry would seek to add to the work already going on and not replace any traditional, tried and tested programmes. Once the missing ingredient of physical activity is added, then sports ministry can be in place to reach the unchurched folk as well as hold on to the youth and men already in attendance.

Christians in Sport run summer camps in England, Scotland, Wales and Northern Ireland. A church sending young people to these camps would see tremendous benefits to their youth work in the returning changed lives.

3. Faith sharing

It is not easy for Christians to share their faith and give the reason for the hope they have (1 Peter 3:15) when they are not socially interacting with unbelievers. A sports ministry framework, however, provides an ideal setting for this to take place and is also instrumental in building up trust and enabling relationships to reach the life sharing level. Dr Greg Linville in his time as Director of Sport and Recreation Ministry at First Friends Church in Canton, Ohio, noted how this framework gave Christians an outstanding opportunity to model not only good sportsmanship but also Christian conversation and values. The manner of their speech, the friendliness of their approach and the interest in their new friends were all attractive qualities that reflected the inner work of the Holy Spirit.

4. Joy of physical activity

When people are relaxed and enjoying themselves there is a tremendous openness and potential for relationship building. In an atmosphere where stress is at a minimum, there are great opportunities for friendships to be forged long term. This can be for many who struggle on the verbal and cerebral front their 'route one' into church. Indeed, their development in this area as disciples and possible leaders, could easily build up confidence for other areas and could soon see them leading house groups, mission teams and Sunday services.

I hope you have been able to glean from this chapter how sport and recreation ministry can be the church's most exciting venture to date. Accepting the challenge will see a dramatic increase in those giving their lives to Christ and, with this, a new enthusiasm for all round ministry by the church. Having physically healthier members within the fellowship at the same time will be one of the many worthwhile by-products of such a ministry.

Having established the biblical basis, cultural relevance and practical feasibility of sport and recreation ministry, the next step is to make a start with it in the local church. The bid has been prepared; it is now time to build the stadium.

3

BUILDING THE STADIUM

> Well-defined goals very quickly expose activities that are hindering progress toward certain objectives
>
> John Maxwell

If you want to be part of a successful church sports ministry then there are eight guidelines that you will find helpful:

1. Receiving the Vision
2. Imparting the Vision
3. Setting the Goals
4. Building a Team
5. Developing a Programme
6. Promoting the Ministry
7. Maintaining the Ministry
8. Turning the Dream into Reality

1. Receiving the Vision

For any ministry to be significant in the Kingdom of God it has to be the result of a calling and not the grasping of an opportune moment. In his book *The Call*, Os Guinness records the words of the nineteenth-century Danish thinker, Søren Kierkegaard, on this subject: 'The thing is to understand myself, to see what God really wants me to do; the thing is to find a truth which is true for me, to find the idea for which I can live and die.'

The local church is God's agency for this age, and for any potential leader of sport and recreation ministry in this setting the first requirement must be a God-given vision. Too many activities have started as bright ideas in an ad-hoc fashion and, being purposeless, have duly petered out with little or no result.

To balance outward activity and busyness with spiritual growth is the number one discipline for the sports minister

The focus must be on God and his heavenly plan right from the start. To think as he thinks, we must be in close communion with him in our prayer life and in our Bible reading times. Sports people do not always find the contemplative life an easy one because they are by nature activists and energetic in their make-up. To balance outward activity and busyness with spiritual growth is the number one discipline for the sports minister. The former clamours for social interaction and frenetic activity, whilst the latter demands individual reflection and solitude. The two must run together, however, if God's gifts are to be maximized and there is to be no divide between the sacred and the secular.

Use a journal to record God's leading

There have been a number of times in my own life when I have sought to distinguish calling from opportunity. One of the most significant was when I was faced with the decision of taking early retirement after thirty years of teaching.

Inspired by Gordon MacDonald's best-selling book, *Ordering Your Private World*, and the words of Habbakuk 2:2a, 'Write down the revelation and make it plain on tablets', I began the process of writing a journal. Whenever I felt that God had something to say to me through Scripture, godly people, circumstances or inner thoughts, I wrote it down. I sometimes went a few months between jottings but then I might have a veritable avalanche of exciting words and sentences. Every six months or so I would review the journal record and use a highlighter pen to pick out the 'calling' thread. It was on the morning of 18 November 1994 that I received from God what I now believe to be destiny scriptures in Ezekiel 17:22–24. I was in my office at school reading my Bible before the day took me over. I had already tendered my resignation to the governing body of the school, and Judith and I were still having nights when we woke up in a sweat wondering what the end of the academic year would bring. It was at this point that Ekeziel intervened:

'This is what the Sovereign LORD says: I myself will take a shoot from the very top of a cedar and plant it; I will break off a tender sprig from its topmost shoots and plant it on a high and lofty mountain. On the mountain heights of Israel I will plant it; it will produce branches and bear fruit and become a splendid cedar. Birds of every kind will nest in it; they will find shelter in the shade of its branches. All the trees of the field will know that I the LORD bring down the tall tree and make the low tree grow tall. I dry up the green tree and make the dry tree flourish.

'I the LORD have spoken, and I will do it.'

I just love the scriptures that begin with the phrase, 'This is what the Lord says.' Such passages have my attention immediately, and Ezekiel 17 was no exception. I was appointed in March 1995 by Christians in Sport to head up their new sport and recreation ministry department in the UK, and in the intervening years I have been excited to see these scriptures unfold year on year. My vulnerability, the increasing visibility of Christians in Sport nationally and internationally, the growth of the church sports ministry 'tree' and the many opportunities to share the vision abroad with 'every kind' of people have all been spin-offs from this commission. The latest link being the emergence of Higher Sports as an eight-week coaching and teaching resource for churches, but more of that in a forthcoming chapter.

That morning in my school office was the undoubted confirmation of God's call into this exciting area of ministry. To use Gordon MacDonald's phrase, it was a time of 'recalibration of the spirit' when one is able 'to pause amidst the daily routines to sort out the truths and commitments by which one is living'.

Stay focused

For the God-given vision to stay in focus we need to do more than safeguard our communion with God. We need to

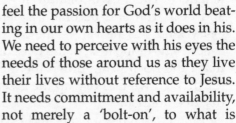

feel the passion for God's world beating in our own hearts as it does in his. We need to perceive with his eyes the needs of those around us as they live their lives without reference to Jesus. It needs commitment and availability, not merely a 'bolt-on', to what is already a busy life. Hands are required on the plough and looking back is not an option. The work is to be viewed to completion and the leader called of God must be ready to stay the course.

In my journal on 6 May 1993, I noted this description of a visionary from Steve Chalke:

A visionary is someone with a dream and a passionate determination and strength of will to make their dream come true. A dream without action floats around in your head and eventually evaporates without ever becoming visible. A dream with action is called vision. Vision gets out of your head and into your hands and feet. Vision changes the way you spend your days, the way you spend your money, the decisions you make, the things you do . . . it changes you.

If God has given you the vision of sport and recreation ministry in your local church then look out! . . . It will change you and your church big time. If ever there was a ministry to get the vision out of your head and into your hands and feet then it has got to be sports ministry. It is where the world is and where the sporty Christian needs to take the life-changing message of Jesus. What a privilege to be Christ's ambassador in the area where we feel so much alive and excited.

2. Imparting the Vision

So, you have the vision for sport and recreation ministry in your church. What is your next step? Don't assume that fellow Christians and church leadership are going to stand back in amazement at your personal revelation. For them to endorse and embrace God's call on your life you will need to impart the vision.

The leadership may include the minister or pastor, elders, staff and people of influence. These are the people who will 'bottom line' the work and if they are worthy of their position you will find them asking some hard questions. Foresight and thoughtful planning can only help in the presentation of your case and in considering any possible negative scenarios. If you start with the premise that the leadership likes you and wants to reach the local community with the saving message of Christ then your whole approach can be upbeat.

There may be an evangelism or mission team in operation already, so your role will be to lay out a modus operandi within the existing system. Suggesting a task force to look at the whole concept of sport and recreation ministry in the church would not be a bad call. This task force would be led by the visionary and would include leadership and interested members of the fellowship. The ideal time for this task force to meet would be over a weekend and if this could be arranged you would know that the church meant business with the ministry. Failing that, a day together would also give the right amount of credence to the new proposals.

3. Setting the Goals

The danger for many churches endeavouring to set up a sport and recreation programme is that they never make the link between the organized activity and the Christian message. They lurch from activity to activity under the misapprehension that sharing an activity with non-Christians is sufficient credibility for the work to progress. This can only be the case if the activity itself is a part of a wider scheme of things and contained within your 'statement of purpose'. Such a statement should encapsulate the philosophy of the entire sports ministry work.

When I was in charge of a large physical education department in a Yorkshire comprehensive school I always operated within the confines of my 'scheme of work'. This embraced every aspect of the department and clearly set out its aims, objectives and methodology. It allowed for regular reviews and appraisals of the progress being made so there was no danger of getting off track.

A statement of purpose is composed along similar lines and is the directional, motivational and inspirational tool for any sports department within the local church. It encapsulates the vision, sets the parameters of the ministry and ensures that the work progresses in tandem with the church's own mission statement. It would, of course, be important to clarify the latter before beginning to compose the former.

Overarching any statement of purpose would be the components of relationship, fellowship, evangelism and discipleship. Every aspect of the statement would be located within the sphere of influence of one or more of these key components.

The following Statement of Purpose covers all these components:

i. Overall values

Sport and recreation is not separate from the church and its other activities. It is an integral part of the total ministry of the church. The spiritual growth aspect makes it different from secular sport and recreation. It gives opportunities to share Christ with others who do not have a personal relationship with him and will help develop spiritual growth in those who are already Christians.

Two verses from 1 Corinthians recording the words of the Apostle Paul are key to this ministry:

> 'I have become all things to all men so that by all possible means I might save some' (9:22).
> 'So whether you eat or drink or whatever you do, do it all for the glory of God' (10:31).

ii. Key objectives

- Provide evangelistic opportunities.
- Strengthen family life.
- Influence the physical health of the individual.
- Provide a setting for spiritual growth and development.
- Plan an all-year-round programme to involve all ages, from children to the active retired.

Churches in the USA are particularly focused on their sports ministry goals and the following extracts give something of a flavour of these:

Germantown Baptist Church, Tennessee
- To help reach and hold young people.
- To enhance the total ministry of the church.
- To help provide families with personal contact and participation as a unit.
- To help break down social barriers.
- To provide activities which allow lifetime participation.

Bethel Church, San Jose, California
- To teach Christian values, build Christian character and develop specific skills in the sports and recreation area.

- To sponsor and/or send out sports teams to develop relationships through their sports that will allow them to be witnesses for Christ.

Grace Community Church, Sun Valley, California
- To provide a godly alternative to children's sports leagues.
- To develop leaders.
- To activate numerous non-involved church members.
- To penetrate the secular sports leagues with a church team.

First Friends Church, Canton, Ohio
- Seek to encourage each participant who does not know Christ to establish a personal relationship with him.
- Seek to inspire a deeper walk with Christ for those who do have a personal relationship with him.
- Seek to communicate a proper Christian ethic of sport and competition to participants in our programmes and also to others who are involved in sport throughout the world.

Greg Linville, when Director of Sports Ministry at First Friends, could not over emphasize the importance of a statement of purpose and believed that it should be on all communications, brochures and registrations. Difficult decisions concerning the ministry could also be weighed by using it as a guiding principle.

First Friends also communicate their statement of purpose more concisely through a motto and a logo. In a word or short sentence, a motto expresses the aim or ideal, whereas a logo gives a visual expression to the same. Some examples of First Friends' mottos are:

'Fit for the King Aerobics'
'More than Conquerors through Christ'
'Go to Grow'
'Overwhelming Victory'

At the end of the day, a statement of purpose is there to make sure that activity for activity's sake doesn't become the rule of thumb. The establishment of kingdom goals and biblical priorities will ensure that the department stays true to its vision.

Rodger Oswald, in his booklet *Sports Ministry and the Church*, is at pains to emphasize that before a sport and recreation ministry can be integrated into the local church there needs to be a 'careful, logical and discerning strategy' in place. To this end, he recommends that the ministry needs to be led by 'the right person with the right passion, co-ordinating the right planning'. He continues his alliteration by then stressing the need to recruit and train 'the right personnel, to produce the right programme which is carefully promoted and diligently moderated through the right procedures'.

4. Team Building

Once the church leadership has recognized the 'call' of God for the establishment and consequent development of sport and recreation ministry, it is then incumbent upon them to set aside those committed to the vision and philosophy of such a ministry. This would be a core team with proven leadership skills and led by 'the right person with the right passion'. The co-ordinator or director would be responsible for pulling a team together with complementary strengths and varied skills. If the foundations are already in place and the commitment and enthusiasm of potential leaders are sufficient, it may be that certain activities should carry their own sub-teams.

Recruitment

The core team would be responsible for the direction of the sport and recreation programme and would be expected to carry out regular reviews concerning its progress. The formulated statement of purpose would always provide the backdrop for this developmental process.

Coaches and officials would be another very important group to pull together and give an identity in their own right. An ideal scenario would be for this group to meet regularly for fellowship and encouragement. Sharing their experiences of Christian coaching and learning from others would be an important facet of the ministry.

Finally, the appointment of a support team would serve to underpin the whole of the work. Their areas of responsibility would include prayer, financial matters, clerical tasks, transport and maintenance. The effective working of this group would give the other two teams the opportunity to practically deliver the programme.

Training

Having set all the teams in motion, the ongoing requirement would be that of training. For any vibrant ministry it is essential to communicate the vision constantly and make room for personal stimulation. A one-to-one discipleship programme sits very naturally in this set up, as do regular team training sessions. Levels of responsibility and account-ability are to be agreed on with appraisal at regular intervals. Teaching on athletic and spiritual integrity would also be central to such a programme.

Some churches in the UK are seeing the distinct advantage in sending team members away on courses to improve their coaching and athletic skills. This is proving to be money well spent from the church's outreach budget and moves the church out of the 'amatuerish' bracket. It is always a bone of contention with me that some folk get away with slapdash efforts at church when they must realize that the same level of performance in their secular job would be far from acceptable.

Christians in Sport runs camps in England, Scotland, Wales and Northern Ireland for teenagers, but the first weekend of every camp includes intensive training for both leaders and coaches. A church sending young men and women as leaders on these camps would profit greatly from the experience they gain.

There is so much good practice going on in other churches that it becomes almost criminal to remain insular

A final but crucial part of the training programme is attendance at retreats and conferences. Not only is this great for team spirit and camaraderie but external input from experts in this field gives new lifeblood to the individual and to the work, as does the opportunity to share experiences with other delegates. In fact, there is so much good practice going on in other churches that it becomes almost criminal to remain insular and even denominational. So many churches have taken years to re-invent the sports ministry wheel when they could have easily taken outside advice and moved at a greater speed.

5. Developing a Programme

The next step to be taken when initiating a sport and recreation ministry is the development of the programme itself. Because this is so crucial to the whole set up I am devoting the whole of the next chapter to the design and implementation of an all-year-round programme.

6. Promoting the Ministry

Role model the ministry

Most churches are slow to change or to accept anything different. They need to be convinced that sports ministry works. Judith and I worked with a small chapel in Cumbria for their sports outreach weekend where attendance at morning service was less than twenty-five, and it dipped even more when the family with eight children went on holiday! They were a fellowship with a heart for the community but had not seen any significant breakthrough. A key part of the weekend was to be a family sports afternoon on a field belonging to one of the chapel members. A friendly public address system, music for the occasion, hay bales, water slides and a refreshment tent all contributed to an event that saw most of the village turn out. This was then followed by a sports quiz in the local community centre and an opportunity to present the gospel. The next day, Sunday, started with a breakfast in the community centre, followed by a sports service. We left a church no longer unconvinced about the effectiveness of sport and recreation ministry.

Inspire the church

There are many avenues to be opened up if you are hoping to get people's attention from the outset, stimulate interest from all the age groups, cultivate a desire to support the programme and release action from the body of the church.

Positive promotion from the pulpit and church leadership will be key to early impact. You will have sold the vision at an earlier stage to those responsible for the direction taken by the church, and this is now payback time. The ministry will only flourish if the church leadership gets solidly behind it.

As the head of a physical education department, I always devoted a significant slice of my time to displays and notice boards. Match reports, coming events and fixtures, team and action photographs, quote of the week and training hints were all ways of keeping the rest of the school up to date and stimulated regarding the sports department. It was also essential to keep the displays fresh and neat so that they received daily scrutiny from those who passed by. A keen photographer on the staff was happy to attend many sports events and then feature them graphically on the display boards. There is no reason why the sports department of a church shouldn't adopt a similar pattern in the entrance porch or church hall so that the visitor is immediately aware of all that is going on in the church's sporting life.

Such displays, together with video footage, could be used for promotional evenings. Special guests, individual invitations, drinks receptions and demonstrations could all be part of this particular promotional approach with attractive offers for those signing up early on the advertised courses.

Advertising through as many channels as possible is equally crucial. Go about this in a business-like fashion and cover every possible angle. Outlets would be the church newsletter, local paper, local schools, billboards, letterbox drops, as well as special invitations to individuals. If you have marketed your activities well and they are immediately popular, you may want to deal with registration on the promotions evening. It is worth covering all this ground in the early days of your sports ministry so that the community is fully aware that there is a new thing coming.

Finally, churches can be inspired by good media coverage. My experience is that the religious correspondents for most newspapers and TV networks are always keen to discover fresh and eye-catching news. An 'Over 60s Aerobics Class', 'Dads and Lads White Water Rafting Weekend', 'Under 6s Football Coaching Clinic', ' Family Sports Day' and 'Go-Karting Evening' are all public interest items that are extremely photogenic and throw up a whole lot of interesting quotes. You might even get a regular spot in some publications and this will come in useful when wanting to advertise the next round of activities.

Inform the church

The danger for any sports ministry is that it can become self-indulgent and start to operate as a separate unit for the benefit of the few. This only serves to fracture its statement of purpose and drastically reduce its effectiveness. Its lifeblood comes from being a grafted branch of the church and producing fruit for the benefit of the whole vine. For this reason it must regularly communicate pertinent information to the rest of the church so that prayer, practical and financial support

Its lifeblood comes from being a grafted branch of the church

remain high on the agenda, keeping the ministry healthy and

active. The litmus test would be to take occasional straw polls of a handful of regular church members and ask them to comment on the work going on and how effective they think it is.

7. Maintaining the Ministry

Stay on track

The whole purpose of goal setting is to keep the ministry focused and within established lines. *We are always better at things inspected than expected* We are always better at things inspected than expected, and it is no bad thing to regularly assess the progress of the ministry against the backcloth of the original statement of purpose. Bright ideas, impetuosity and 'ad hoc' activities usually falter because they don't have this discipline written into their planning.

Never stint on quality

If you plan to be professional in all that you do, then you will find that quality leads naturally to quantity. Rodger Oswald of Church Sports International recommends a seven-point plan to churches as they seek to be at their best for God:

1. Adequate and safe facilities.
2. Durable and sufficient equipment.
3. Kit for both short-term and long-term use. Planned obsolescence where necessary.
4. Integrity with your schedule – stay with dates and times first planned.

5. Competent coaches and officials. Where possible, train your own so they can have a spiritual as well as an activity ministry.
6. Parity in competition. Where numbers allow, start the course with a rating clinic and then draft the players so there is equality in the teams.
7. Start your administration well and keep the standards high.

Communication

This needs to be of a high standard within the ministry team, the church as a whole and into the wider community. Promotional evenings, registration times, team selection, schedule announcement and special events, all need wide cover through clear channels of communication.

Evaluation

There is no place for 'inner sanctum' evaluations. The real picture will only emerge if the evaluation is quantitative. To this end, there needs to be an involvement of all participants – coaches, officials, players and parents. Only then will the core team gain some understanding of the direction in which the work is going and whether the set goals are being met. A policy of appraisal and accountability within the core team will provide excellent back up to the quantitative evaluation result.

Protection of the competitive environment

Any church sports ministry department should have an enviable reputation for the high standards set in a competitive situation. In an age when officials are frequently lambasted for their decision-making, it is important for the principles of integrity, honesty, accountability and fair play to be laid down from the start and then honoured throughout. There is also a need to clarify the way consequential actions will be dealt with. In this way, the unacceptable action can be met with the agreed discipline in order that the proper restoration can then take place. The opportunities to pull the atmosphere of heaven down onto the earth's playing fields are endless and must be sought after with impunity.

Pull the atmosphere of heaven down onto the earth's playing fields

Appreciation

During a large portion of my teaching career, I served under a headmaster who never took your contributions to the life of the school for granted. He would notice when I had followed a full day's teaching with an after school coaching session, before spending the rest of the evening involved with parent-teacher interviews. To arrive home at 10 p.m. after an 8 a.m. start was very much part of the job as a teacher on numerous occasions. However, it only took the briefest of memos from the headmaster the next morning, expressing his appreciation for my long stint, to keep me on track and enthusiastic for the day ahead.

Any ministry, sports or otherwise, will maintain its health if built around a determination to affirm its contributors and use any and every opportunity to thank and praise where appropriate. Thank you notes, memos, flowers, phone calls and meals out are all building blocks in this process.

Rewards

Where these are appropriate, it is worth considering whether they need to be perishable or imperishable by nature. A trophy may be good for certain occasions whereas a ticket for the 'big game' or an afternoon dry slope skiing would suit others. For the level of awards it may be best to look out for 'most improved', 'most inspirational', 'best leader' as well as 'most valuable player'. However, too strong an emphasis on awards is not to be encouraged.

Keeping records

Building up a good database of every participant in the various programmes is very important and can have such long-term consequences. A notification letter to someone on the books who you have not seen for a few years can prove to be very timely in God's plan for their lives. This is also useful should you decide to have an annual sports dinner and want to invite every person you have had any contact with.

8. Turning the Dream into Reality

Os Guinness in *The Call* has a chapter on 'Dreamers of the Day', where he identifies such people as those who 'respond to the gap between vision and reality by closing it'. He goes on to say that Christian vision 'is an act of imaginative seeing that combines the insight of faith, which goes to the heart of things below the surface,

Strategic planning is required with any sports programme if reality is to be injected into dreams

with the foresight of faith, which soars beyond the present with the power of a possible future'.

Strategic planning is required with any sports programme if reality is to be injected into dreams. The visionary needs to constantly ask questions of himself and his core team as he seeks to turn his vision into a realistic destination. A good place to start is to make an accurate assessment of the starting point, with an understanding of the resources that are available. As a useful template the following five questions will help to keep the programme in good shape:

1. *Where am I?*
   Make an accurate assessment of your starting point and the resources that are available. 'Here', of course, is the only realistic place that you can start from.

2. *Where do I want to go?*
   Always identify your goal and be certain to begin your journey with the end in mind.

3. *How am I going to get there?*
   It is vital that you set your objectives, plan your route and map out your pathway. However far ahead you have set your sights, the only way to get there is one step at a time.

4. *What is my timetable?*
   Be realistic with deadlines. Reasonable and clear deadlines help you to assess more easily whether you are on target. To come out with a statement like 'as quickly as possible' only serves to make the deadline unclear and is virtually un-assessable. Draw up a 'critical path' – a detailed schedule of deadlines.

5. *How am I doing?*

Many great ideas have failed because this vital step has been ignored. It is important to constantly evaluate progress against objectives and the critical path which has been established. Meet regularly with others to assess this progress. A monthly appraisal sheet can be a very useful document in this respect.

There can be no doubt that goals and objectives help our faith to flourish. Praying for a whole village to be won for Christ is one thing, but setting a goal to work with young mums and their children in a tiny tots gymnastics programme and then organizing an evening fitness circuit with the dads, actually turns prayer into reality. Not only that but it lets the church and the community know that God is at work.

If you are answering God's call when you begin your sports ministry then you can equally call on God for the success of this same ministry: 'Call to me and I will answer you and tell you great and unsearchable things you do not know' (Jeremiah 33:3).

God has much to reveal of himself and his ways in sports ministry. Hold this promise before you as you explore your personal vision and consider all the ramifications of starting a sport and recreation ministry.

4

PROGRAMME
OF EVENTS

Two things come to mind: the community has a need and the
local church requires the resources to meet that need
                                                    Dr Greg Linville

For a church to embark on a sports ministry programme it
makes sense to have a long-term plan in mind to enable the
community to see that there is something both reliable and
consistent in place. This also makes it possible for an enquir-
er to see at a glance what activities are running for the next
six or twelve months and know what will be of personal
interest. Careful planning is required if the needs of all age
groups in the community are to be met. The fixture list
should be put together with much prayer and planning.

The immediate danger when planning a programme is to
be guided by the interests of the core and coaching teams
rather than by the needs of the community. I'm not advo-
cating here that extreme sports or deep-sea fishing take
precedence over football and aerobics, for example, but
rather that the planning team has a sensitivity to where the
people in the community are at with their sport and recreation activities.

Research the Community

A demographic survey of your community is a great place to start. Key questions must be answered:

- What sporting and recreational facilities are already in place?
- What coaching/activities are being done well and appear to be well attended?
- What age groups and gender are already being catered for?
- What facilities can be hired to augment the facilities already possessed by the church?
- What sports are being offered by the local schools? Who are they reaching and are they doing a good job?

Take a walk around your community and plot the facilities – leisure centres, sports halls, community centres, village halls, tennis courts, football fields, green areas, hard court areas and so on. Do not try to replicate what is already very popular and being done well, unless you have a large group that would prefer a less intense, but not less professional, set up. That then leads you on to gleaning the sporting and recreational interests of those who are already part of your fellowship, remembering to play to the obvious strengths.

Take a walk around your community and plot the facilities

Research the Church

Your 'in house' survey will be more effective if you fully consider the following tips when distributing a survey sheet:

- Give a brief 'selling the vision' talk before the survey sheet is issued for the congregation to fill in.
- Pick a Sunday service when the survey can be given the highest priority by the church leadership.
- Don't let the exercise get lost in the usual morass of notices.
- Ideally, make time in the service for the completion of the survey. Give it out at the door on arrival and distribute pens at filling-in time.
- Make it as easy as possible to fill in with tick boxes and yes/no answers.
- Collect the survey sheets in immediately after completion.
- Distribute spare copies afterwards to any regular attenders that happen to be missing on the day.

You are looking for a number of key facts from this survey:

- Where the sporting interests of the church members are to be found.
- What they are happy to participate in with their friends.
- Whether they would be prepared to coach or officiate.
- What technical skills they would be prepared to offer (computing, clerical, administrative).

A few weeks after the survey has been completed it will be important to report back to the church on the results. Overhead projection graphs or PowerPoint presentations will serve to give advance warning that this ministry is organized, efficient and to be taken seriously.

Identify your resources

Whatever comes from your community and church research, one thing is sure – your progress will need to be linked with resources. From the outset, you should work within these resources and, as you get established, you can then start to stretch yourself and think bigger. Finances, facilities and personnel are vital to your resource planning.

Finances

People are used to paying for their sporting and recreational pleasures so that gives you a good start. You are not embarking on a ministry that will exert excessive strain on the church budget, so that will keep church leadership happy. However, it will be important to agree on the contribution the church should make out of its outreach budget. If we believe that the church is a group that also exists for the benefit of its non-members then this policy should go through without contention.

You are not embarking on a ministry that will exert excessive strain on the church budget

There are many ways that the sports ministry team can supplement financial support and so guarantee the continuing growth of the ministry. Coaching sessions and courses should carry an approved fee that will go towards equipment and the hire of facilities and officials. Certain members of the church, because of their support and interest, could be approached for designated giving. You may want to establish a '20 Club' or '100 Club' of these special people depending on the size of your church and enthusiasm of its members. Again, the way you have already sold the vision will determine the success of this venture.

Sponsorship is another area to investigate. A local business may be happy to provide such items as shirts, balls and aerobics mats, especially if you can persuade your local newspaper to mention the business when reporting on your latest activity or sports result. Marathon and half marathon runners are always looking for good causes in order to make their ordeal satisfying. What better cause than running for the local church and its sports ministry work in the community.

Government grants are also a possibility for churches that spearhead youth work in the community. In socially deprived areas, the successes of sporting and recreation activities speaks for themselves and are seen to be making good use of government money. Sports Pursuits is an organization led by Derek Jefferson, ex-professional footballer with Ipswich Town, who works in the inner-city area of Birmingham. It has had some rave reviews from head teachers as a result of its work with disaffected young people.

Facilities

A complaint often heard in the UK, though not so much in the USA, is that the church has no facilities to effectively run a sports ministry department. It is true that churches with fields and sports halls are in a small minority, but the wealth of facilities around most churches is largely undiscovered.

a) Public fields can be turned into impromptu football pitches, family fun days and sports competitions.
b) Local schools will have halls, gymnasia and sports halls that can be hired at very reasonable costs. If the church has good connections with its local school then there may be no cost implications at all, especially if the children from the school are profiting from the programme being run.
c) Sports centres are in abundance in the UK and even have executive suites for that special occasion.

d) The church hall or even the church itself can be a great resource facility. All too often, the former is hired out to a secular sports group and the latter handles an average of two to three hours of activity in a whole week! Chessington Evangelical Church had the right idea in the late 1990s when it constructed a purpose-built church that doubled up as a community leisure centre during the week. Given the name 'The King's Centre' it became the church at the heart of the community. The large carpeted sports hall could take several badminton and volleyball courts as well as providing a full-sized five-a-side football arena. On Sundays, the chairs are put in place for a worship area that takes around a thousand people. The key factor with Chessington's sports ministry is that the church has control over all the week's activities. This enables the spiritual dimension to be introduced into the programme alongside the coaching and teaching skills. Hiring your church hall out to the local short mat bowls club takes away that opportunity completely.

The church at the heart of the community

Personnel

Leadership personnel are obviously quite crucial to the programme and a good mix of talent and coaching skills is desirable. However, the best-planned programme won't break any records if there is an absence of participators. In this respect, it is essential from day one to educate the church in a 'you and who' campaign. There are always some who see the activities merely in place for their own personal pleasure, with a little fellowship thrown in for good measure. On the contrary, a sport and recreation ministry is chiefly in place for those who aren't Christians in order to serve them in the community and, at the same time, introduce them to Jesus. A 'you and who' campaign fits the bill nicely for these objectives. The Christian, when subscribing to a programme or an event, should always think double. Who can I invite? Who can make up my team? This policy also introduces ownership to the sports ministry programme from those participating, and helps deliver the statement of purpose. It also serves to accelerate the ministry and bring others into the Kingdom of God.

Designing a 'Fit for Purpose' Programme

In designing a programme to suit your clientele, it is essential to be aware of the many people groups that you will have in the community: children, youth, adults, singles, couples, active retired, men, women, people with special needs.

It is with all these groups in mind that the following subsections come into play:

1. Recreation and leisure

Under this heading you may find that a board game evening catches the imagination or a 'Question of Sport' quiz. Both can be rounded off with a small supper and an appropriate devotional. With a number of churches, for 'Question of Sport' evenings, I have used a video of a Christian athlete as part of the quiz and then picked up on one of the points made during the video to expand on the gospel. *The Ultimate Goal* video, produced for football World Cups, has the testimonies and playing highlights of leading international footballers. The footage on each footballer takes around eight minutes and is ideal to play between rounds or during an interval slot. Christians in Sport has moved this outreach resource up several notches in the past two years with their 'A Question of Sport Quiz'. They have used it 700 times in churches around the UK and have trained twenty-five speakers across the UK to deliver it. Friday nights are particularly popular with club and recreational players since it sets the scene for a good weekend's banter of the quiz on its opening night, as well as enabling them to devote all day Saturday to their sport. This very professional quiz is Christians in Sport's key strategy for churches with the 2012 Olympics in mind and in their partnership with More Than Gold.

2. Fitness

This is an area where the church must have a view and a strategy. Judith and I live in a small village in Wensleydale, North Yorkshire. Here, and in all the nearby villages, there are pilates, aerobics, circuit training and aqua-fit classes. Those attending demonstrate a wide range of fitness and an even wider range of shape and size. Teenagers and the active retired flank these groups that include every other age group in between. It is a great place for the Christian to be and, thus far, Judith has had some great conversations with other ladies she has met at these classes, a number of whom have come to special outreach events held in the village. With regard to the local church running its own fitness classes, I look at this aspect in the following chapter, 'Beyond the Boundaries'.

3. Outdoor activities

Jogging and walking clubs provide good opportunities to spend time with people over a lengthy period and the activity can be tailored to suit the needs and abilities of the members. The jogging can range from 2 to 3 mile stretches around the town or countryside, to running as a team in a half or full marathon for a worthwhile cause. As relationships are forged, one of the weekly sessions could take the form of a light meal at one of the runner's houses and then be followed by a Bible study on the 'Race of Life' (see details of this study in Chapter 10, 'Passing on the Torch').

Having a keen walker in your church can be a real blessing

Having a keen walker in your church can be a real blessing, especially if this person is also a knowledgeable naturalist as well. If numbers grow quickly for this activity, then it makes sense to grade the walks to suit all levels of ability. Some of my deepest conversations with men have been whilst undertaking a steady ridge walk in Swaledale during an annual outdoor activities residential weekend. Such occasions provide quality time, when real life issues can surface and the good news of God's Kingdom can be shared.

An annual camping week or weekend for church members and their friends is another activity that is worth including in your yearly calendar. As well as the fun and frenzy of being together, there will be countless opportunities for morning devotionals, camp fire sharing and home-grown Sunday services. Again, play to the strengths of your members and allow the keen campers to plan this kind of event with you.

Rock-climbing, caving, canoeing and back-packing are all specialized outdoor activities. However, many of your friends might be delighted to participate in them. Use local expertise where you can, although you could have a Christian outdoor centre within reasonable travelling distance. Evening talks and devotionals on these occasions flow naturally from the challenges that the day has brought forth. Stuck on a rock face and being guided to safety by 'the one who knows the way' is a powerful analogy of the salvation available in Jesus. Not that I'm suggesting that you contrive cliff-hanging situations in order to get home your point!

A final outdoor activity worth a mention is fishing. This activity has a greater number of participants than any other sport in the UK. It is more individualistic than the previous activities mentioned, but the time travelling to the river or sea and then the 'après fish' occasion can all be worthwhile times with friends and acquaintances. It wouldn't be too hard to find New Testament parallels for this activity when the time came for a devotional together.

In all instances, the key is being creative. When Keith McIntosh, Health, Safety and Environment Officer at Manchester United, found that a number of unchurched dads were keen on deep-sea fishing, he organized a 'dads and lads' fishing trip from Fleetwood on the north-west coast of England. It was an opportunity to deepen friendships in a non-threatening atmosphere and to look to God to prosper the situation.

4. Leagues and tournaments

Once you have decided which team games, if any, you are going to include at sometime during the year, the next step is determining the form of the activity. I shall use football as an example, but in its place you could easily substitute basketball, netball, cricket, field hockey, street hockey, rugby, short mat bowls and so on. The chosen game could be played at several levels in your sport and recreation programme.

- Occasional five-a-side evenings in the local sports hall for church members and their friends with the emphasis being on fun and friendship. If the surroundings allow it, a short message or discussion could take place at the close of the activity. If the church has its own playing area then this may be easier to arrange.
- Joining a five-a-side secular league as a complete Christian team. The emphasis now is on the teams you play and you will need to decide on a strategy in line with the objectives you have set in your sports ministry. You may want to start and/or finish with a prayer huddle, give out sports tracts to your opponents, demonstrate the fruits of the Spirit in your playing performance and use the physical skills God has given you to the best of your ability in a competitive situation. Go out of your way to develop strong friendships with the teams you play and, where appropriate, invite them to an outreach event (they could enter a team in your 'Question of Sport' evening) or to your end-of-season dinner.

Go out of your way to develop strong friendships with the teams you play

- Enter your eleven-a-side team(s) in the local secular league. My advice here is that the majority of your team are Christians. Any non-Christians must be fully at ease with the reasons why you are playing in a secular league – to play competitively yet 'christianly' and to share your faith. They must also be prepared to maintain the standards of play and behaviour agreed upon.
- Enter your eleven-a-side team in a Christian league. Here the emphasis can be on the non-Christian players who should still make up the minority of the team (never more

than four would be my suggestion). The organizers of such leagues should seek to maintain at all times the standards that honour God and enable all the players to express their footballing skills. Midweek training sessions could include light but meaningful Bible studies and all games could start with prayer and, preferably, end with prayer. The end-of-season dinner and presentation evening should always be seen as an opportunity to share the vision of the team and the hope of the gospel. Your keynote speaker does not have to be a famous sportsman but does have to be a good communicator using a sporting context. A brief interview with one of the Christian players is also recommended. Molesey Community Church, under the guidance of Mark Blythe, provides a brilliant example of how this type of league can function. Read more about Mark's 'Sports Force' ministry in Chapter 8, 'Sports Ministries at Home and Abroad'.

- Taking a team on tour can be a natural progression of a successful programme. The dynamics of this can be found in Chapter 1, 'Firm Footings', under the heading of 'The Church Team'. I was privileged to be the manager of a Christians in Sport rugby team that briefly toured Northern Ireland. As well as producing a very high level of rugby, with wins over Carrickfergus Rugby Club and Queens University, Belfast, the team members had an opportunity to share their testimonies in church and at the rugby club, as well as playing a significant part in the various community events arranged around the tour. Daily morning devotionals led by the tour chaplain, Tim Bryan, served to both encourage the Christians in the team and challenge the non-Christians.

- Residential tournaments can offer an extra dimension of intensity and deeper fellowship. To play several games during the day and then relax in the evening with colleagues and opponents alike, can provide numerous opportunities for sharing the Christian life. A magazine-style presentation after the meal could contain video footage of the day, an interview with a Christian referee and a sports quiz, all before a short punchy talk from a good communicator. Breakfast the next morning might contain a 'thought for the day'.

- Five-a-side tournaments can attract many entries and are not difficult for the church to run. Players love to participate in a well-organized tournament that runs on time and is clear about the standards it expects. For details of how to plan, run and follow up such a tournament, see Chapter 5, 'Beyond the Boundaries'.

- Resources must be a key consideration if you are serious about forming a church team. Do your homework first:

  ■ *Be certain how many others are interested in playing and what their availability is. Start in a small way so that you can assess the ability level and detect long-term enthusiasm.*

  ■ *Check on your local facilities, both for their cost and availability.*

  ■ *Consider the price of kit and equipment as well as the officials' fees.*

  ■ *Form a wise management team to consider such items as match fees, transport costs, captain and coach selection, constitution, etc.*

5. Events

You may feel that your church is not ready yet for a full-blown sport and recreation ministry programme but would respond positively to the occasional event. Indeed, the success of the occasional event may cause the leadership to seriously consider a regular programme and, even later, a sports minister.

The Sports Personality

It must be pointed out at this stage, however, that a well-known sports personality is not required to make the event a success. You may feel that the personality may encourage more of your friends and neighbours to come along, but the ultimate test will be their interest in the activity and the strength of the relationship they have with you. Always work on the premise that sport and recreation are the drawing factors – they will still be around when the well-known personality has left town.

There are, of course, occasions when it is right and proper for high-profile athletes to communicate their faith in Christ to as wide an audience as possible, and you may find there are times when this kind of partnership will work as an integral part of the whole ministry. It is incumbent on each and every Christian athlete to role model the gospel in both their performance and their lifestyle. They can be ambitious, and when this ambition is firstly for God's glory rather than their own, then their impact on the sporting world can be immense.

It is incumbent on each and every Christian athlete to role model the gospel in both their performance and their lifestyle

Each Christian athlete has to work out how he or she can use the gifting God has given them and how they can 'complete the work' they have 'received in the Lord' (Colossians 4:17). It must never be forgotten that the first call on any Christian athlete, after their personal walk with God, is to the colleagues they regularly work with. In their very specialized secular sporting environment, the Christian message may only be evident in their lifestyle.

Henry Olonga is a fine example of the Christian athlete using his gifting for God's glory. As the youngest and first black player to represent Zimbabwe at cricket, he came to the world's attention with his black armband protest that proclaimed the death of democracy in Zimbabwe during the 2003 Cricket World Cup in South Africa. His autobiography, *Blood, Sweat and Treason* (2010), charts God's grace in his life and reveals how he is using the window of opportunity given to him through his sports personality status to share his faith in Christ.

Planning the Event

You will do well to address the following questions for any event you hold:

- What is the purpose of the event?
- How much pre-planning is required?
- What will be the event programme?
- How will I follow up the event?

This maxim could apply equally to a large sports dinner or to having a few friends around to watch a World Cup football match. As part of a wider programme, planning it against the backcloth of your aims and objectives would be a useful exercise.

Judith and I followed the above guidelines for an outreach event in our Wensleydale village. The purpose of the evening, entitled 'Faith and Sport', was to invite friends and neighbours to a convivial gathering in a village hall where Christian athletes would be interviewed about their sport and how they integrated it with their faith. The pre-planning had started some weeks before with a barn dance, at which personal invitations were issued. Good quality posters and invitation cards were then distributed around the village and surrounding areas, as well as arranging for a preliminary write-up in the local paper. The village hall was booked in good time and had been checked for seating, amplification and the heating system, since it was late November! The booking had allowed for a full hour before the event took place in order to cater for any last minute panic situations. The evening started with drinks and nibbles on arrival, with tables set out restaurant style to give an informal feel to the occasion.

The three guests were interviewed in a very informal style and shared much of what Jesus meant to them and how he was central to their ambitions in sport. The chatty nature of their presentations meant that their listeners could extract the information that met their present needs without feeling they were being 'spoken at'. The open question time at the end of the interviews revealed something of the impact their testimonies had had on the packed room of people.

At the conclusion of the question time, a team had prepared coffee, tea and cake to be distributed to the tables and it was a good forty-five minutes before people realized they had homes to go to. There had been no charge for the evening, to ensure maximum attendance, but the opportunity to donate towards costs revealed a generous spirit from many. Clipboards in strategic places requested address details from those who wished to be informed of similar events in the future. Many names went down on these sheets, and a follow-up system was put in place.

Variety, the Spice of Life

Over recent years the following church-organized events have been brought to my attention: golf days; 10K and fun runs; football clinics and courses; five-a-side football competitions; sports outreach weekends; outdoor activity weekends; sports breakfasts and dinners; family sports afternoons; 'It's a Knockout' competition; swimming pool party – 'It's a Washout!'; Christians in Sport's 'A Question of Sport Quiz'; sports centre activity sessions (basketball, netball, football, hockey); tenpin bowling; short mat bowls; church teams in football, cricket, rugby, netball, hockey and basketball; mini-Olympics; World Cup football, cricket and rugby events – big screen showings, breakfasts, dinners, tournaments, Sunday services to name but a few!

This chapter has sought to inspire you to get on with sport and recreation ministry by identifying the needs of your church and community before beginning to design your programme. I have tried to present you with the foundation blocks for setting up any kind of programme, be it a one-off event or an all-year-round fixture list. The choice of activities is endless but each activity must be planned within your overall goals, and as part of your church's vision and mission statement. Should this be the case then you will begin to see a real growth in your church as your local community is opened up to the things of God and the people of God.

5

BEYOND THE BOUNDARIES

The Celtic strategy of sending teams into 'enemy territory' is
the greatest 'apostolic adventure' available to Christians today
George G. Hunter III

A temporary measure is to give a man a fish in order to sat-
isfy his appetite. A lasting solution is to teach him the skill
of fishing. Jesus set this principle in motion when he assem-
bled his evangelistic team on the shores of Lake Galilee. The
twenty-first-century church must follow his example if it is
to go beyond the church boundaries and meet with people
in their everyday activities.

Sport and recreation ministry in the church will have no
great effectiveness if it takes on the guise of the occasional
fish used as an appetizer. So many churches believe that
sports ministry is down to inviting a well-known sportsperson to speak to a packed congregation. The reason is usually a laudable one, in that the testimony of a sporting role
model will encourage many to consider choosing the
Christian life. Whatever the reason, it is rare to find such an
invitation as part of an ongoing sports ministry programme
but rather the result of a bright idea at a church meeting or
having a good contact in the sporting world. The end result
tends to be a faithful presentation of the gospel to a good
number of people but with little thought given to follow-up
and continuing sports ministry outreach.

Now, don't hear me wrong on this issue. It is absolutely crucial for the talented and well-known sports personality to use every opportunity to share Christ and to give a reason for the hope that is within. In an earlier chapter, I quoted the words of Mordecai in Esther 4:14b when he intimated that Esther's elevated position into sovereignty had prepared her 'for such a time as this'. For a short span of time, the national and international athlete has a window of opportunity and a platform for the gospel that will not occur again. The special gifting received from God enables this person to role model the Christian life in a sporting world sadly bereft of biblical standards and integrity. To acknowledge where that gifting has come from and to give God the glory for it is one of the most powerful witnessing tools present in the modern world.

If you have been carefully following the text, you will think at this stage that I have just reduced my initial argument to ribbons. I hope, however, that you can see the difference between the use and misuse of the sports personality. All too often the church has been guilty of a 'media' approach that serves to elevate the personality almost above their humanity and brings undue pressure as a consequence.

Strategy

Any fisherman will tell you that there are many ways of catching a fish and many types of fishing rods to accomplish this task. Sport and recreation ministry is no different, and the rest of this chapter is devoted to working out plans on how to use different activities to both serve people's enjoyment and present the challenge of new life in Christ. The list is not exhaustive and the activities themselves can be easily tweaked to suit your situation and clientele. All I ask is that your planning and preparation finds a place within the vision of reaching your sports community for Christ. Only then will it stay on track and not become one of many disparate measures employed by the church. Note that I said disparate and not desperate!

The common denominator in all this, however, is that of the church being prepared to leave its comfort zone and venture beyond its boundaries.

SPORTS OUTREACH WEEKEND

During our time with Christians in Sport, Judith and I were involved in over fifty such weekends with different churches up and down the United Kingdom and one in Russia! Whilst the overriding aim has been to reach the local community with the life-changing message of Jesus, the methodology has varied from church to church.

- For some churches the weekend has been an integral part of their year-round programme, enabling them to invite their many contacts to specific tailor-made events, culminating in a sports celebration and outreach service.
- Other churches have been praying and planning over a sport and recreation ministry for some time; the weekend serves to 'kick-start' that into action and bring the ministry to the attention of the rest of the church. It is important that those who doubt the relevance of sports ministry within the church get plenty of opportunity to witness its effectiveness.
- Finally, there are churches for whom such a weekend is a whole new venture. They have racked their brains over the years as to how they can be 'salt and light' in their

communities and begin to make a difference in everyday living. In many cases, these churches have contacted sports ministry organizations, usually with a high-profile athlete in mind, only to be introduced to the potential of their own home-grown sports ministry.

The ingredients of a sports outreach weekend are not limited to a specific age group. A typical programme may pursue the following direction:

Friday evening – the church young people invite their friends to join them for an evening of frenetic activity and an appropriate devotional. See later in the chapter for specific ideas like mini-Olympics.

Saturday morning – sports breakfast with an appropriate after breakfast sports speaker and/or video. This can be followed by a training seminar for members of the church who are either involved or being called to this ministry.

Saturday afternoon – a sports jamboree for all ages, indoors or outdoors depending on the season. Allow for a brief interview or testimony at the half-time break.

Saturday evening – sports quiz and buffet. Video extracts of Christian sportsmen and women to be included in the quiz or shown between rounds whilst the marking is going on. Allow space for a gospel presentation within a sporting context by a good communicator. This should last no longer than 15 minutes.

Sunday morning – an all-church worship service. The style of service must be aimed at the interests of the irregular attendee or non-churchgoer. A magazine-style approach often goes down well with drama, interviews, modern songs, video, brief Bible readings and short but punchy talks. All those who have attended the activities on Friday and Saturday should be invited to this centre point of the weekend's activities.

Sunday afternoon – mainly a 'chill out' time for all those who had worked hard to make the weekend a possibility. However, a debriefing session can be useful whilst every-thing is still fresh in people's minds. High on the list for this session would be planning for follow-up and Christianity Explored or Alpha-type courses.

Sunday evening – where churches have evening youth services, the theme of physical and spiritual challenge could be continued. The involvement of sporting Christians would be essential here, whether by interview, testimony or talk. A sports studio or changing room background would put the service in a modern frame.

A number of churches we have worked with have used all seven of these weekend slots but many have chosen to con-centrate on a small handful. I've certainly found seven talks in forty-eight hours to be challenging! Creativity knows no bounds when God is at the planning stage.

OUTREACH DINNER

Purpose

To provide a non-threatening atmosphere where friend-ships can be forged, food enjoyed and the gospel presented in an attractive and challenging way.

Pre-planning

- Identify your target group – football team, peripheral church members, work colleagues, teammates, neighbours, etc.
- Select an attractive venue. A neutral location is better than church premises if the budget allows, e.g. local sports centre or sports club, restaurant or nearest league club's hospitality suite.
- Charge a price that will enable Christians to bring their friends without having to take out a second mortgage. However, the meal and the evening do need to have a 'first class' touch. The church may be happy to pay for the venue and the literature from its outreach budget, whilst individuals could have the opportunity to provide bursaries for those who are keen to bring friends but can't afford to pay for them.
- The guiding principle for attendance at such functions always needs to be 'you and who?' Think double!
- If you plan to use a public address system then be sure to have a competent person on hand to make it work.

The event

- Allow a 15–30 minute reception period before the programme starts officially. This can set the atmosphere for the evening as drinks and nibbles are made available.
- A cold starter already on the table rather than hot soup will save time.
- Have quality sports/Christian literature on hand so that folk can browse through them during the reception period.
- Select a good master of ceremonies to link the evening together. This person should welcome everyone officially

from the front after the reception and then give a brief overview of the evening's programme before giving thanks for the meal.

- It is best to complete all the courses before any of the speaking starts. This gives time for the tables to be cleared by staff. It is important that there are no distractions for the speaker.
- If you want some variety to your presentation then an interview with a Christian sports person about the inter-relationship between their sport and their faith could precede the main speaker. Equally, an appropriate 5-minute video extract could be included before or during the talk.
- Where possible, arrange for the caterers to bring a second cup of tea or coffee after the talk. This enables conversations to take place about what has been said, as well as allowing time for response cards to be filled in.
- Remember that a high-profile personality is not essential for the success of this occasion.

Follow-up

Always have another event lined up and, where possible, have details to give away at the dinner. Think in terms of ongoing ministry rather than a one-off event.

FIVE-A-SIDE FOOTBALL COMPETITION

Purpose

To bring friends, neighbours and workmates into a well-organized sporting environment where there will be an opportunity to play good football and hear about new life in Christ.

Pre-planning

- Begin early with your planning – two to three months is ideal. This gives time for the required facilities to be booked and for the teams to be put together.
- Decide on the number of teams. Set a deadline for the return of entry forms. These are to include names and addresses, team colours and non-returnable entry fees. A good working number would be eight teams – if there is an international competition in progress at the time then use the names of the seeded teams. Squads of seven would cover injury problems and increase your outreach numbers.
- Plan for entry fees to cover the cost of the sports centre booking. Prizes – trophies, T-shirts, sports New Testaments – could be paid for from the outreach budget, as could the cost of souvenir brochures for all the participants. These are always available from Verité Sport every two years for the occasions of the European and World Cup competitions – www.veritesport.org.

The event

- A programme of events must be visible in several areas to guarantee that the games run on time.
- Based on one playing area and eight teams, a period of three hours should be allocated. Two playing areas would cut down this time considerably.
- Arrange two pools with the teams playing every other team in their pool. The positions after three rounds would lead to the following pairings:

  4th place Pool A v 4th place Pool B
  3rd place Pool A v 3rd place Pool B
  2nd place Pool A v 2nd place Pool B
  Winners Pool A v Winners Pool B

- All games to be of 6-minute duration with 30 seconds allowed for half time and substitution.
- Organize two good referees, suitably dressed and taking alternate games. If you had two playing areas they may be happy to referee without a break, even though this is not ideal.
- A 15-minute break needs to be structured into the session for drinks and a short talk.
- The presentation is to take place after the game between the two pool winners. Encourage all teams to stay for the final and close the occasion with a prayer of thanksgiving.

Follow-up

It is always helpful if the participants can receive an invitation to a future sports ministry event – sports breakfast/dinner, sports service, big screen showing, big game party – so that the contact you have established with them can be maintained.

INDOOR TOUCH RUGBY COMPETITION

The template for the five-a-side football competition can also be applied to rugby with the following supplements. Book the local sports hall or school gymnasium for the evening and set up an all-age and both-gender competition. Women's rugby is one of the fastest growing sports in the UK today.

A few tips:

- Select sides of five, six or seven players depending on the size of your playing area.

- Play across the width of the arena and not from end to end.
- If a player carrying the ball is touched, then the ball must be passed immediately. Failure to do so gives the ball to the opposition.
- A score involves the ball being touched against the wall whilst still in the hand.
- Restarts simply involve the ball being passed whilst the opposition must be at least 5 metres back from where the ball is being played.
- Have a short coaching session at the start of the competition if there are those who are playing rugby for the first time.

SPORTS SERVICE

See Chapter 11 'More Than Gold' for details of how to plan and deliver a sports service.

MAJOR SPORTS EVENT

Such is the enthusiasm for sport throughout the world that a year does not go by without a major international tournament of some kind taking place. The Olympic Games, World Cups in football, cricket, rugby and athletics, as well as the Commonwealth Games, have all captured people's interest and imagination in recent years.

As already mentioned and outlined, competitions, meals and services can be built around these major events. Other ideas that have been successful are as follows:

Major event 'party'

The lead for this activity has been given for a number of years by Christians in the USA. The American Football Superbowl final becomes the talking point for the whole country, and a special video featuring Christian players is produced by sports ministries for use by individuals or groups when watching the final together.

In the same way, recent Football (soccer) World Cups have led to similar endeavours throughout the world. As well as showing the video before the game or at half time, the hosts provide food, drinks and appropriate literature. On such occasions, a video and souvenir brochure called *The Ultimate Goal* was used extensively in many countries. These resources can be used in tandem with watching the game on a big screen in the church hall or at a local community centre. Further details of this kind of occasion can be found in Chapter 11 'More Than Gold'.

Mini-Olympics

The Olympics and the Commonwealth Games are ideal opportunities for the running of a competition under the 'More Than Gold' theme (1 Peter 1:7 KJV and CEV) and then concluding with appropriate spiritual comparisons. Several sports can be included, outdoors or indoors, and in large or small areas. Each activity is timed and a point allocated every time it is successfully accomplished. An ideal team number is five, although any number from three to seven will keep everybody constantly active. Experience has shown that 3 minutes per activity gives everyone in the team several attempts to register points. With larger teams, the time allocation could be increased. Ten separate activities will enable you to cater for between thirty and seventy young people or adults. Some examples of the activities are as follows:

- **Football:** score by side-footing the ball to hit a cone or by dribbling round cones before returning to your place.
- **Rugby:** zigzagging between cones or touching the ball down on the outward run and then picking it up on your way back.
- **Hockey:** dribble between cones to the end of the line before speed dribbling back to your team.
- **Basketball:** speed dribble or a zigzag cone dribble. Set shooting when a basketball ring is available.
- **Frisbee:** throw beyond a line where the Frisbee has to be caught to record a point.
- **Tennis:** run with racquet out in front of you whilst bouncing the ball up and down on the racquet face or run with racquet and ball and play the ball into a large container at the end of the run.
- **Badminton:** serve the shuttlecock and land it inside a hoop on the floor.
- **Bowls:** roll the ball to stop between two parallel lines on the floor.
- **Cricket:** throw a tennis ball to hit the wicket.
- **Croquet:** hit the croquet ball with approved action through an arch.

The environmental conditions will require some of the activities to be adjusted from time to time. If you are outside on a windy day, the badminton option may need to give way to a second football activity. Frisbee throwing may not go down so well in a small enclosed space, though it would be fine in a sports hall.

If you have more teams than activities, you can always combine two teams together per activity with one keeping the score whilst the other competes.

All team members keep in strict rotation whatever their ability. This ensures maximum effort from all taking part and no domination by a few.

From an organizational stand point, the teams should be instructed to stop all activity on the whistle and bonus points can be awarded for the first team to line up straight. One member then reports to the competition scorer with their team's tally. By keeping a running total and announcing scores at regular intervals you will keep all participants on their toes.

Before the awards ceremony (bronze, silver and gold medals together with a special award for 'top effort', perhaps to the youngest team) the teams can be gathered into a central area for a short talk. A coloured 'gospel' rugby ball or football (black, red, white, green and gold) can be used as a visual aid to explain God's plan of salvation.

OUTDOOR ACTIVITIES WEEKEND

For over twenty-five years now, I have been joining men at a residential centre in the Yorkshire Dales for an outdoor activities weekend. Marrick Priory in Swaledale is an ideal centre for establishing a balance between physical and spiritual activities, and over these years many men have deepened their Christian faith, whilst others have come to know Jesus personally for the first time. There is a lot to be said for removing folk for a brief period of time from the traffic lanes of life to a place of tranquillity in order to give them thinking time and spiritual refreshment. An American colleague of mine leads an annual expedition of families to the shores of the Great Lakes for similar reasons. No sport and recreation ministry programme is complete, in my view, without a week or weekend of this nature.

The planning of such a weekend should be guided by the Christian content of the party. My plan is always to balance the weekend in the direction of those who had not entered into a personal relationship with Christ at that point in their lives. The invitation letter, however, must pull no punches and make it clear that the programme includes both spiritual and physical challenges. In fact, in most cases I have entitled the weekend 'The Marrick Challenge'.

Let me take you through a typical Marrick programme so that you have something of a backdrop to any future plans you may hatch.

Friday evening

With people leaving work at different times, a relaxed and flexible buffet meal starts the weekend off. This is followed by a 'nightline' activity on the surrounding hillside. In half-light, teams are roped together and blindfolded. They then work their way around a rough terrain course reliant only on the person in front for instructions – 'low branch on your left', 'deep pothole to your right' would be typical calls. This exercise is the best one I know for dealing with groups coming together for the first time. Bonding is swift and every individual is immediately a significant member of the group. The late-night fellowship following the nightline is usually around a guitar with a 5-minute talk to introduce the theme for the weekend. The experienced members of the party then know to hit the dormitories quickly and get some shut-eye before the snorers take over!

Saturday morning

A full English breakfast always proves to be as good a preparation as anything for the customary Fremington Edge walk. The morning walk is such an excellent time for relationships to be forged and new people made to feel part of the group. It is an opportunity for deep and serious conversation with those who prefer it, as well as allowing ideal preparation time for hearing God's voice over the weekend.

Saturday afternoon

Here the Centre staff come into their own and offer instruction in a myriad of activities – climbing, gorge scrambling, caving, kayaking, mountain biking and orienteering. Each one is challenging in its own right and provides each individual with plenty of conversational mileage over the coming months. Plunging into subterranean streams below ground only takes your breath away the first time!

Saturday evening

The indoor climbing wall, mass rotational table tennis and the Marrick darts championships are all facets of the evening programme before a lengthier fellowship time. By now the group has gelled and, as well as the singing reaching gusto proportions, a number of the party are anxious to share their day's experiences and what they have learnt about their walk with God. These testimony times are fresh and relevant to the non-Christian men in the group and the concluding talk seeks to complement the spiritual mood of the evening. Conversations over a late-night drink are always significant.

Sunday morning

The chapel at Marrick seems to have been a gathering place for God's people over the centuries. The early Celtic saints would have described it as a 'thin place' where heaven and earth come close to touching. To have a bunch of men in the chapel from all walks of life singing their hearts out has got to be experienced to be appreciated. The sun invariably casts its rays through the chapel windows and has marked, for many over the years, the start of a new life with Jesus. Communion and ministry combine together so naturally and few can leave the chapel in any doubt that God has turned up in style. So as not to give any scope to the sacred/secular divide, so endemic in the church of today, the after-service coffee is usually followed by archery and antics on the ropes course, both places where God can be enjoyed and worshipped.

Few can leave the chapel in any doubt that God has turned up in style

I have never been disappointed with any Marrick weekend and would like to think that I will be going there for many more years to come and continue to be thrilled by the advent of new life. There may be a time coming soon, however, when the Saturday afternoon gorge plunge is given a miss in favour of a power nap and listening to the football results!

AEROBICS

It has been a privilege for Judith and me, on two of our outreach weekends with churches, to work with Rosemary Conley, the aerobics 'guru' of 'hip and thigh diet' fame. On these occasions, Rosemary was able to demonstrate the significant role that aerobics has to play in any sports ministry programme.

Although not exclusively female, aerobics classes do tend to attract women rather than men. In many ways the word 'aerobics' has been hijacked because the accepted 'father of aerobics', Dr Kenneth Cooper, never intended it to be linked solely with a particular type of movement class. The word itself means 'living in air' or 'utilizing oxygen' and refers to breathless activity that causes the heart rate to be raised into the individual's target zone, which is usually between 65 per cent and 85 per cent of their maximum heart rate. Maximum heart rate can be calculated by subtracting your present age from 220. Anaerobic exercise is that accomplished 'without oxygen' and simply means that the activity is performed without utilizing the oxygen that you are breathing. It will come into play beyond the 85 per cent mark and is another ball game altogether. Serious athletes would include a fair degree of anaerobic exercise in their training programme.

By returning to aerobics as an activity class, I shall, for the purpose of this book, disappoint Ken Cooper. Should this text fall into his hands – I should be so lucky – then I would seek his forgiveness, at the same time as telling him that his series of books over the last three decades around the subjects of aerobics, preventative medicine and fitness, have been an undeniable source of inspiration to this disciple of Jesus and physical education.

Rosemary Conley's approach to her outreach aerobics class provided a good blueprint for churches wishing to install their own programme. The following characteristics were demonstrated:

- The class had been well publicized and the Christian ladies had worked hard at inviting their friends. Rosemary Conley was an obvious attraction but, in the fitness age in which we live, there is little difficulty drumming up a group of folk to join you for such occasions.

- Everything was run in a professional manner and the level of fitness was gleaned from the participants at the outset. This determined the programme to be set. Regular checks were then made on the progress of the class during the work out, with plenty of opportunities for water intake to prevent any dehydration.

- The music used was Christian worship style that served to introduce Scripture verses and understanding.

- After the appropriate warm down, Rosemary gathered the group around her and shared about her personal journey in becoming a Christian. She told how God intervened at a broken time in her life and relationships, and how spiritual and physical fitness have become God's gifts for her to share and communicate with others.

A regular church aerobics class could also use personal testimony in its programme but a 'thought for the day' or a 'teaching point' might be more common on a regular basis.

It is important that the class begins to see the interrelationship between physical and spiritual fitness at an early stage

It is important that the class begins to see the interrelationship between physical and spiritual fitness at an early stage.

Many churches are beginning to think seriously about sending one of their members on a course to receive the appropriate qualifications. A two-week course, or several weekends, may well cost around £300–£400, but it would be money well spent by a church serious about sport and recreation ministry. It is essential that all teachers are fully qualified and that a check is made to see that the church insurance policy covers the activity. It is also vital that the person getting qualified is a mature enough Christian to be able to teach the rudiments of the Christian life and be equipped to lead enquirers to faith in Christ.

First Friends Church in Canton, Ohio, has issued the following Statement of Purpose and goals for its aerobics classes:

1. To provide opportunities for instructors and assistants to develop relationships with their classes so that they can experience the claims of Christ in a non-threatening, non-forced environment.
2. These relationships should give the instructors opportunities to: (a) share their faith (b) disciple (c) develop friendships (d) communicate a Christian ethic of exercise.
3. To provide encouragement for those who may feel 'old' or 'out of shape'.
4. To show unconditional love and acceptance to everyone, but particularly those who feel unloved or unaccepted because of the way they view their bodies.
5. To provide each participant with the message that Christ loves us just as we are and that in our weaknesses his strength is made perfect (2 Corinthians 12:9).
6. To provide each participant with a positive experience in exercise.
7. To encourage participants to set small and reachable goals and help them to achieve those goals.
8. To provide this service to the community regardless of a person's race, creed, age or church background.

'QUESTION OF SPORT' QUIZ EVENING

This has proved to be one of the most successful recreational outreach events. These evenings have been held in church halls, schools, working men's clubs, sports centres, village halls and many other venues. Without fail, they attract a wide age range of people and, having been the 'after quiz' speaker at a countless number of these evenings around the UK, I can offer up several tips from the good practice observed:

- Select a master of ceremonies who will have a natural rapport with the audience.
- Having a 'picture round' sheet on each table as folk arrive serves to get everybody into team mode fairly quickly.
- Christians are encouraged to make up a team from their friends, neighbours, teammates, colleagues at work or family.
- A sports video between rounds with some light Christian content helps as a preparation for the keynote speaker.
- If a supper/meal is to be included, then this comes best at the halfway point. This should then be followed with a lively 10- to 15-minute evangelistic message from the speaker for the evening.
- Response forms and invitations to future events can be placed on the tables after the talk, together with suitable sports tracts.
- Some churches have included a few non-sports rounds for those whose knowledge of sporting facts is not extensive.
- The winning team can be presented with sports New Testaments as well as the usual quiz-type prizes.

FAMILY SPORTS DAY

Purpose

This is fourfold:

1. It gives the family time together and helps to strengthen family life and relationships.
2. It uses competitive activities as a means of producing an atmosphere of fun and enthusiasm.
3. It enables the church to reach out to people who might not accept an invitation to church in the first instance but will have no problem joining you for such fun activities.
4. It will provide a bridge with unbelievers and open up opportunities to build relationships and open the door to sharing faith in Christ.

Pre-planning

- Pick a date and facility in good time.
- Order a PA system and check its set up capability.
- Design invitations and posters.
- Advertise in the church bulletin from six weeks before the event and then at weekly intervals.
- Posters to go up with five weeks to go.
- Announcements to Sunday schools and local schools four weeks before the event.
- Start registering the participants from three weeks before the event.
- Flyers in church bulletin and through letter boxes two weeks before the event.
- Give personal invitations to all your friends and acquaintances.

The event

Helpful hints to ensure your family sports day goes off successfully:

1. Have your team leaders lined up before the event so that you can double check on all their responsibilities. It is essential from the starting whistle that everybody knows they are attending a well-organized event.
2. The number of teams will depend on the names on your sign-up sheet. Make certain that equality reigns both for numbers and age groups. Keep families together. As the participants arrive, send them to their 'team pen' where they are greeted by the team leader and assistant. When each team is complete, a team name is chosen democratically and a team cheer invented and practised.
3. Plan your events with different age groups in mind. Start with a few events that are less strenuous and can act as a warm up to the more energetic ones later on.
4. Ideally, try to have a coach with each event to explain and supervise.
5. Keep the scoreboard ticking over after every event. The team cheer can be used at this stage to maintain enthusiasm, and extra points can be awarded by the organizer for the non-competitive hallmarks – helping an injured teammate, leaving the equipment in a tidy state for the next team, having the best team cheer, showing remarkable team spirit.
6. It is often good to take a break in the middle of the event for drinks and refreshments. This would also be a good time to introduce your speaker. A local athlete could talk about competing as a Christian, or one of the dads might share about the difference Jesus makes to a family.

7. The master of ceremonies (MC) is a key figure who should keep the show on the road with enthusiasm and humour. To facilitate this, make certain that the public address system is efficient and in good working order.

8. Don't let the day operate differently from its title. It is a time of fun not over-zealous competition. Keep on top of any cheating that goes on. You might be dealing with Christians but some see red mist where competitions are concerned.

9. If you decide to have a 'Parent and Son/Daughter Day' make certain that men and women without children can adopt any spare children. This does wonders for community relationships.

10. Try to give out as many prizes as you are able – winning team, fair play award, best team spirit, and so on. Have a chocolate bar and a drink for everybody at the end.

11. The way you close the event is crucial. Be sure to thank the guests for being there and those from the church who made it all possible. See that everyone receives an invite card to church and any similar events. Particularly stress the next family occasion.

12. Bring the clean-up team into operation. Don't just rely on that gifted group of people who always stay behind to be helpful.

ORGANIZING A GOLF DAY

Golf days present wonderful opportunities for the Christian golfer to enjoy the company of friends and colleagues and present them with the reality of the Christian message. Golf is such a popular sport and it is amazing how many folk have a set of clubs even if they don't play regularly.

A typical day's programme might be as follows:

9.30 a.m. – arrival and coffee
10.00 a.m. – morning competition
12.30 p.m. – soup and sandwiches
2.00 p.m. – afternoon competition
7.30 p.m. – evening meal, prize giving and guest speaker

Note: if you are planning a golf day for the first time, you may want to keep the day down to one round of golf plus the meal.

The above programme is based on a day consisting of twenty-seven holes of golf and, therefore, should be near to where most people live, and should not be a strenuous walk. It is probably only practical to organize a day like this during the week, as it may be virtually impossible to get on most golf courses for these times on a Saturday. Another disadvantage to organizing a golf day on a Saturday is that most courses are closed to visitors until late morning, which makes organizing anything more than eighteen holes difficult. Also, for family men and women it is not always a good idea to block off the whole of a Saturday for golf.

There are considerable advantages to holding the event during the week:

- It is easier to book a good golf course.
- If people book a day's holiday from work, there is less time pressure on them than at the weekend when domestic duties may call. In this regard, there will also be a greater take up to stay for the evening meal.
- Businessmen can take the opportunity to invite contacts.
- It is easier to book a good speaker.
- Most courses will be cheaper to play during the week than at the weekend.

Organizing the event locally also has advantages:

- Spouses can be invited to the evening meal and this tends to elevate the tone of the evening.
- The non-Christian target audience is, potentially, doubled.
- The likelihood of guests coming for the golf and then leaving before the meal is reduced.

For the afternoon competition, it is good to play the better golfers together. This means that the morning competition can enable hosts and guests to play together over nine holes. It is important, however, to decide on what sort of competition you want to play, and make sure you know the rules governing the competition. Confusion over who the eventual winners are can be a major irritant to your guests.

It is always difficult to select teams from individual applicants, so it is much better if people can be encouraged to get together a team of either two, three or four.

Planning

Find a golf course that will accept a block booking and make sure you negotiate a price that takes into account green fee, dinner, sandwich lunch (if required) and the use of a private room with a public address system. It is usual, but not necessary, to give all players a 'goody' bag (e.g. a couple of balls, tees and a chocolate bar) so this needs budgeting for as well.

Produce an invitation that makes it clear that the golf day includes the dinner. Do not accept entries from people who will not attend the dinner. The invitation should also make it clear that it is a church sports ministry event, since it is important that everyone knows what they are coming to.

Specify the deadline for payment – last minute entries can easily confuse your planning. Ask if people have someone with whom they particularly want to play. Be sure everyone knows when the day begins and enclose a map of how to find the course in a confirmation letter to all entrants.

The day needs to be billed as an outreach opportunity for bridge building and sharing the gospel

It is not always easy to get people to commit to a golf day so you need to plan well in advance. Experience shows that it is less easy nowadays for people to get time off work than it used to be, a strong argument for making the event very attractive. Publicize the event regularly in your church bulletin and hand out flyers. If you can get twenty golfers and another ten or so guests for the evening meal, then you are well on track. Obviously, an entertaining speaker can add to the appeal and help with support. The day needs to be billed as an outreach opportunity for bridge building and sharing the gospel.

Finally, it may make sense to steer clear of a club that requires handicap certificates since most golfers on an average church day will not be golf club members. All players, however, should be reminded of any dress code that may be in operation.

Cost

For a midweek booking, you may be looking at any amount between £35 and £50. It would be more for a weekend. Green fees for a day could be £25 with coffee, soup and sandwiches, whilst the evening meal may vary between £10 and £15. On top of this, you need to consider your prize fund and the expenses for your guest speaker. Obviously, costs can be trimmed, usually by the selection of the course and facilities you choose. A good marker for your eventual choice would be the opinion of the regular golfers in the church, since they are likely to form the core of supporters at the event. Don't forget that you want an attractive venue for the evening meal.

On the question of cost, why not ask the church for some help towards the speaker's expenses and the give-away literature from Christians in Sport. Church members may also be happy to help towards a little bit of sponsorship for the prizes.

Prizes

A quality first prize for the individual competition is a must, together with prizes for the winning team in the morning. For the afternoon competition, it would be good to have prizes for the 1st, 2nd and 3rd teams, as well as one for the longest drive and nearest the pin. A hole-in-one would not be allowed to pass unnoticed either! Limit the prizes to one per person and have a few light-hearted ones thrown in – 'best effort', 'shot of the day', etc. With a bit of forward planning, it is amazing how you can gather prizes with a relatively modest budget.

On arrival

A registration table should be set up in a convenient and obvious location. Each player should be given clear instructions for the day – tee off time, card of the course, local rules and details of the format. The 'goody' bag provision will add a favourable impression. You might include a sports tract on a well-known golfer.

Coffee should be available and members of the organizing committee should welcome everyone and field any questions. Name badges for any 'key' people would be useful.

The play

Ensure that a starter is present on the first tee; a shot-gun format (where everyone starts at the same time, one group on the first tee, another on the second tee, etc.) has the advantage of having everyone start and finish at the same time. If this format is used then ensure that the gun is fired from where it can be heard by everyone. This type of start usually means the course has to be closed to the public so you may have to resort to a two or three tee start.

Avoid slow play by urging players to 'pick-up' if they can no longer score on the hole. Ensure that at least one person on each team is an experienced golfer, familiar with both the rules and etiquette of the game. This person should be appointed the team captain so that their authority is unquestioned.

After the competition, check the cards as quickly as you can and then post the results on a board in the bar or foyer.

The dinner

It is always best to announce results and present prizes before the speeches. Sensitivity towards the audience should always be a priority and the content of the gospel talk should be carefully considered. The majority of the players may be new to Christian things and would therefore profit more from the gentle testimony of a fellow golfer than a full gospel presentation. If, however, the company is used to sports ministry occasions, then a greater challenge may be called for and, with it, the opportunity to invite Christ into their lives.

Sensitivity towards the audience should always be a priority

A second cup of coffee after the talk allows discussion of the day's activities and any points raised by the speaker. Return slips on the tables can be useful for gaining feedback and interest as well as advertising the next exploring Christianity course.

Something different

A trip to a local golf driving range in an evening can be great fun, especially for people who haven't played golf. The driving range will make clubs available if necessary, and might also provide their teaching professional for an hour or so in order to spend a few minutes with each group, going through the basics of the golf swing.

The party can then go back to church, or some suitable location, for a pizza and a speaker. The cost for such an evening can be quite reasonable and opens up your clientele. Such an occasion could also be useful for getting just the Christian golfers together and then 'selling' them the vision of a golf day.

Final notes

- A number of churches can come together for a golf day if any one church finds it difficult to go it alone.
- Prayer backing is essential for all aspects of the day, even the weather.

- A church golf day can be a stepping stone to the regional and national golf days organized by Mark Blythe at Sports Force.
- If the course is narrow, it would be good to have ball spotters at appropriate holes.
- Always be sure to make friends with the local pro and their assistant. Buying prizes from them will help a lot with relationships and co-operation.

The purpose of this chapter has been to give you a flavour of sports activities that some churches are doing very successfully. They are all very adaptable and can be tailored to suit your individual church situation and needs. It is important, however, that whatever you embark on you keep within the vision and mission statement of your ministry. This will always provide the backcloth to how you are progressing.

You will have been going 'beyond the boundaries' and taking the Kingdom of God to the sports areas of the nation. There is a target audience of 150,000 registered sports clubs and associations in the UK with ten million members. Consequently, for those church members who play in these teams on a regular basis, the type of sports quiz/dinner provided by Christians in Sport would prove to be both popular and ideal as it interfaces directly with the sports culture of our day.

6

THE
ACADEMY

A healthy fit body is the most appropriate home for a vibrant spirit

Dr Kenneth H. Cooper

The world has never been any different. It longs for heroes that it can enjoy, emulate and sometimes even worship. Unfortunately, too many heroes are taken in by their own publicity and, woefully, fall short of the intended target. The talented musician, who is an inspiration to many, finds the world of drugs and compromising relationships all too attractive to resist. The footballer whose shirt and number adorns the back of young and old alike, can't avoid using the field of play for aggressive and vengeful behaviour. Sadly, these gifted people are role models to a younger generation that can't always discern the difference between reputation and character. It is here where the Christian athlete can take over the scoring. To reflect the life of Christ in the world of sport is both challenging and daunting. However, there can be no finer thing than a person living for Jesus in the intense laboratory of the sporting world.

There has never been any dispute over the benefits that playing sport can bring to the life of a young person. The areas of character, relationships, attitude and leadership can be truly honed under the right coach. To combine this with Christian principles and attractive role modelling lays the ground for the development of a mature young person that is going to grow 'in favour with God and men' (Luke 2:52).

Sports ministry has a huge part to play in bringing all this about for the present 'Academy' generation and three specific areas weigh in with strong contributions:

1. Sports Camps
2. Higher Sports Courses
3. Sports Values Series

1. SPORTS CAMPS

In the early 1990s, Steve Connor, an ex-linebacker with the Chicago Bears and the Los Angeles Rams, came to Oxford ostensibly to coach the local American Football team but chiefly to discover what ministry plans God had got in store for him. His whole outlook on life had changed after a football camp in the States where his coach had led him to Christ. Coach Rex remained a significant role model for Steve until his recent death, when Steve delivered the oration at his funeral. Inheriting the same passion for sport and Jesus as Coach Rex, Steve joined the ranks of Christians in Sport and headed up their youth department.

It wasn't long before the concept of an English sports camp came onto Steve's radar. It had been the arena of his own conversion and he had seen so many other lives changed by Jesus at such camps. Consequently, the first Sports Plus Camp in the summer of 1994 took place at Cokethorpe School in Oxfordshire. Thirty young people between the ages of 11 and 17 gathered, with a further thirty from Adventure Plus, the Christian outdoor-pursuits organization.

It was my privilege to be the Dean on this first Sports Plus Camp and I remember the day when Steve and I shared a dream together – for God to so bless Sports Plus that there would come a time when camps were happening in England, Scotland, Ireland and Wales. I don't think either of us expected to see this achieved after only a decade. Steve went on to head up his own organization, Sports Outreach, in Scotland and now in the USA. Leaving Sports Plus in the safe hands of Christians in Sport will arguably be his greatest legacy in the UK as these sports camps go on from strength to strength.

Christians in Sport runs summer camps in all the four home countries for teenagers who are passionate about their sport. Early registration has become a must for those wanting a place, and often England and Wales have to run two back-to-back camps. Coaching is of the highest standard in the major sports of football, tennis, hockey, rugby, netball, athletics, basketball and golf, and is delivered during intense morning and afternoon sessions. An early morning pre-breakfast run around the campus, together with daily Team Challenge activities, serve to supplement all the coaching going on. The leadership team of coaches, team leaders, speakers and support staff is always a large one so that a ratio of two leaders to every three athletes can be maintained. The purpose of the camp is to demonstrate the Christian life in the world of sport so that the young athletes can be challenged to walk that way themselves. For Christian

The purpose of the camp is to demonstrate the Christian life in the world of sport

youngsters, the camp is a time of growth and fresh challenges, whilst for others it is often the very start of their spiritual journey with Jesus.

Talented young men and women in their late teens and early twenties provide role model examples during the week in a variety of ways:

- All leaders and coaches meet for a weekend of training before the young people arrive on the Sunday afternoon. This serves to give a great balance to the camp since these leaders are both receiving as well as giving in the camp situation.
- The early morning run sees a full camp turn out (250–300) with the team leaders and coaches running alongside the athletes.
- A quality warm down and stretching session is followed by a 5-minute testimony from one of the leaders.
- The after breakfast team meeting is an exciting mixture of sports video footage, lively worship songs, pulsating quizzes, interviews and brief but interesting talks, all of which communicate to the athletes the challenging adventure of being a Christian.
- The morning coaching sessions work the athletes hard and always include a devotional break in the middle. This provides a sports value moment for the coach who may choose to look from a Christian perspective at such areas as teamwork, leadership, winning with humility, losing with dignity and persistence. The athletes themselves will also be given an opportunity to share how God is working in their lives. The afternoon coaching sessions would follow along similar lines.
- The daily Team Challenge competition gives the leaders many opportunities to stress and develop Christian character in their respective teams. Seven-minute games of halo, non-stop cricket, ultimate Frisbee, volleyball, rugby/netball and football, for example, contribute to a junior and senior league and help to bind both team and

leaders together. The leaders don't take part in these games but spend all their time on the touchline encouraging and supporting their charges. All games are concluded with both teams forming a huddle for a prayer together. Prayers every 7 minutes on the sports field . . . now there's a revolutionary concept!

- Free time before the evening meal often finds the athletes and leaders trying their hand at different sports and developing friendships.

- The evening meeting is a magazine-style programme aimed right at the heart of youth sports culture with state of the art technology. Loud music, sporting clips from well-known films, on-stage challenging competitions and thought-provoking talks. This is followed by a time in dormitories for all athletes and their leaders in order to study the Bible and discuss the theme of the day, as well as the major point from the evening talk. These times have seen many young athletes give their lives to Christ over the years.

- During the dormitory times, the coaches gather to have their own time together. As well as sharing their experiences of the day, they also pray for the many teams as they meet to discuss the claims of Christ on their lives. The desire of the coaches is not merely to be Christian coaches but to learn together how they might coach 'Christianly'.

By the end of camp, the athletes are beginning to see how the secular and the spiritual life can be as one in the world of sport. The coaches and leaders they have come to admire are constantly at pains to demonstrate the discipline of following Jesus as well as obeying the rules of their sport. Respecting your opponent, showing integrity in your relationship with your teammates, having the right attitude to match officials, coping with a poor performance are all key issues that are more easily appreciated and understood when they come from an experienced coach.

Team leaders continue their contact with the athletes throughout the year with regular correspondence as they encourage them to keep on keeping on in the Christian life and in their sporting development.

Sport is the language that plugs generation gaps and opens up communication channels

Sport is the language that plugs generation gaps and opens up communication channels. The coming together of generations in a sports camp setting only bears out the remarkable nature of this medium. It is fertile ground for the things of God to be demonstrated and embraced so that, as each new generation comes through, there will always be a good crop of those who love their Lord and love their sport. It is the kind of Academy God has always had in mind.

2. HIGHER SPORTS

Seeds of Inspiration

During my appointment as the International Director of Church Sports and Recreation Ministers (CSRM), I spent a lot of time in the States working alongside a number of churches that had strong sports ministry programmes. In many of the churches, I found that a catalyst for growth was a particular programme called 'Upward Basketball'. In 1986, through the vision of a recreation minister called Caz

McCaslin, Upward Basketball began at a church in Spartanburg, South Carolina. Emphasis was placed on Christ-likeness and good sportsmanship. Changed hearts and lives were seen in both those who played basketball and those who administered the league.

With a full gymnasium and twenty-seven children on the waiting list, Caz began evaluating the church grounds to see if anything could be constructed into a basketball court. The estimate for such a project was over $11,000. After sharing his vision with a friend, he was generously given the funds to proceed, and the seeds of Upward Basketball were planted.

When the next basketball season came, Caz was unsure of what to do. He explored the possibilities of building more courts at the church. On approaching his friend who had met his needs before, he was told that he didn't need another gym. Rather, he needed 1,000 gyms! This inspirational comment led to the growth of Upward Basketball from one church to seven churches and now, nearly a quarter of a century later, Upward Sports is the world's largest Christian sports programme for children.

Tremendous growth in the last ten years has taken Upward to almost every state in the USA, as well as forty countries. The basketball ministry has now been joined by soccer, flag football and cheerleading. Each year, some one million people around the world play, coach, referee or volunteer in Upward Sports leagues and camps, hosted by more than 2,600 churches.

Birth of Higher Sports

After regularly observing this exciting church resource in the States, I would return to England constantly wondering how the principles of Upward Basketball could work in UK churches. I was realistic enough to know that basketball wouldn't get many takers but wondered about other national sports.

It was a day in the summer of 2006 when Judith and I were visiting the east-coast town of Filey. We were joined on this occasion by one of our sons, Ben, and his wife, Airlie. Ben had spent his summer after university working with First Friends Church in Canton, Ohio, in their sports ministry department. He had successfully run a church-sponsored rugby and cricket course in the community and, like me, was keen to see the start of something similar in the UK. As we strolled along the Filey promenade, the germination of Higher Sports took place, initially in the shape of Higher Rugby.

A Church-run Sports Course

From the start, the mission statement of Higher Sports was 'to equip the local church to change lives for Jesus through sport' and the following aspects were foundational:

- An adaptable eight-week course that combined sports coaching with Christian teaching and was available to young people of both genders.
- A curriculum that could be followed and practised by the local church without requiring external personnel – we were both conscious that the British church had the mistaken view that sports ministry was something you imported and asked others to do.
- A resource pack that contained all that was necessary by way of coaching and teaching modules, as well as the appropriate kit and sports equipment.

- As well as the Christian teaching module, each pack would also contain a coloured powerball. This would enable the coach to use the colours in explaining about the Christian life. The powerball shape would obviously reflect the sport being coached.
- The teaching material would be based around a biblical role model and placed within the context of sport.
- The Higher Sports pack would be flexible so that it could be used in schools as well as churches. To this end, 'sports values' would be an intrinsic part of the material, enabling it to be taught in a classroom situation.
- There would be flexibility to allow the course to be shortened or lengthened to suit particular circumstances, and to have the ability to run as a holiday club or sports camp.
- Each course to conclude with a presentation ceremony, when achievements can be recognized, prizes awarded and the Christian message clearly proclaimed.

On the strength of these principles, Higher Rugby came into being. Ben was playing rugby at national league standard and was a level three coach, so it was more than appropriate for him to write the coaching drills. He put himself in the place of a coach who enjoyed rugby but didn't necessarily have a coaching qualification. Clear diagrams and well-explained coaching drills meant that the weekly progressions could be easily followed and adapted by local church course leaders. It was to take the shape of 'no contact' tag rugby and, therefore, ideal for boys and girls of all ages.

Alongside the coaching drills, small team games and competition grids came the devotional side. This would take the form of a 'team talk' and could come either during a break in the coaching or at the end of each session. When first trialled in the small Wensleydale village of Crakehall, the playing area was alongside the church. Taking rugby boots off and then coming into church for the team talk was a new experience for the youngsters but quickly became a natural part of the course.

Higher Rugby follows the life of Daniel ('Daniel, a First Team Player') for its team talks under the following subtitles:

- Transfer to the Premiership
- Everyone has a Big Dream
- Coping with Pressure
- Dropped from the Team
- Changes in the Board Room
- In Among the Lions

Powerball

The coach can use the supplied powerball and the following text to supplement the Daniel series. A separate colour could form the basis of the team talk or all the colours could be presented during one session:

Step 1

Using an under-inflated ball that looks inflated, drop it to the ground, demonstrating the fact that it cannot bounce. Ask the following questions:

- What is the problem? – no air, flat
- When the ball's creator made it, what was his intention? – to bounce, to be kicked, to be handled firmly, etc.
- What is required for this ball to fulfil its potential? – to be filled with air

Step 2

Now turn to the inflated powerball with its coloured panels, remembering that the gospel is the 'power' of God unto salvation (Romans 1:16).

Blue: God is a creative genius (hold the ball up and use it as a model for the earth). He created the blue heavens and seas, and surrounded them with teeming life. The earth was placed just the right distance from the sun to prevent it either freezing up or burning to a cinder (move the ball appropriately to demonstrate this). Then came God's special creation, completely different from the rest of the living creatures – ourselves. Like the action required with a deflated ball, God breathed into man the 'breath of life' (Genesis 2:7) and the special relationship had begun.

Gold: God wants this relationship to last right through into eternal life. It's the question everyone asks: 'Why am I here? What is my purpose?' The Bible tells us that the streets of heaven are paved with gold; a lovely picture of what eternity with God is all about and what excitement there is in store for us. God created us to enjoy this special relationship with him while here on earth.

Seams around the panels/Dark: Unfortunately, we've not lived up to expectation – made mistakes, lied, got angry, been selfish, etc. There's a little word that describes these big things spoiling our relationship with God and other people: sin. This causes us to lose touch with our Creator and we find ourselves bound and tied up, just like the seams do to the panels (in the football you can refer to the dark panels and the absence of light). We are prevented from being the people God intended us to be.

Red: Fortunately, God was not prepared to leave us bound up. In an event that split history in two, he sent his son Jesus on a rescue mission to live at our level before paying the penalty for our sins by his death on Calvary's Cross. He knew that we couldn't save ourselves, and the red panel reminds us of the blood that Jesus shed in paying that debt we owed.

White: This colour represents how God sees us once we have said we are sorry for our sins and invited Jesus to be our Rescuer and Saviour. Forgiveness clears away the binding and brings us into a new and everlasting friendship with God. We are lifted 'higher' (hold up the white 'Higher Rugby' words on the ball) by God and are no longer held down by our own selfishness and failings.

Green: Becoming a Christian means that heaven is your future (show Gold panel again) but earth is still your home. The Bible tells us that God has a great plan for each of us and he wants us to grow (show Green panel) in our faith and understanding of what it means to live as a Christian. We find out more about God's plan for our lives as we take time to read the Bible and talk to God in our prayer times. It also becomes important to spend time with other Christians and learn from each other.

Step 3

The final step will depend on the circumstances and the situation you find yourself in when delivering the powerball team talk:

- Have appropriate literature available for interested youngsters i.e. sports leaflet or sports New Testament.

- Suggest future time slots for any wanting to know more about becoming a Christian.
- Make the powerball available to all those who have attended the Higher Rugby course as a constant reminder of God's love for them. It could be the most memorable award they ever receive.

Final comment

You may wish to adapt this talk to suit the young people you are working with. However, it is important to make clear right from the start that Higher Rugby is there to show them how God wants to use the physical gifts they have and how special they are to him. Sharing the good news of forgiveness and eternal life in Christ through the powerball and weekly use of the ball in the coaching sessions will serve as a constant reminder of these truths.

Higher Football

In 2008, a meeting of UK Sports Ministry leaders led to phase two in the development of Higher Sports Limited, which had by then been recognized as a Christian charity. Present at that meeting was John Squires, a key leader with the worldwide football ministry, Ambassadors in Sport. John had noticed the development of Higher Rugby and agreed to write the coaching and teaching curriculum for Higher Football. It followed along the same lines as the rugby resource but with bibs replacing tags, a round powerball replacing an oval one and 'The Life of David' replacing 'Daniel, a First Team Player'.

John is an experienced coach and prepared many leaders in South Africa for ministry during the 2010 World Cup. His progressive drills and small team games are a coach's dream, and I only wish I had had them at my disposal on leaving Loughborough as a young PE teacher. Like the rugby coaching manual, each session is supplemented with clear diagrams and easy-to-follow instructions.

'The Life of David' curriculum is so designed that it can be worked into the coaching session rather than as a stand-alone team talk. This enables 'teachable moments' to reinforce the theme of each session.

The David series has the following subtitles:

- Growing in Obscurity
- Overcoming Giants and Obstacles
- Making Others Great
- Self-Control
- Overcoming Temptation
- Hitting the Target
- Counting the Cost

Higher Games

The final component of Higher Sports is to be Higher Games, now in the midst of production. It will enable churches and schools to run a variety of small team games concurrently and will be ideal for use in the community during the London Olympics and any other international sporting event. Six different sports will be supplemented by the powerball text and teaching material on the 'Life of Joseph'.

3. SPORTS VALUES SERIES

Higher Sports can be adapted as part of a school's Physical Education programme, delivering Key Stage 2 values within the classroom environment as well as forming part of a Religious Education syllabus with extended studies of the team talk material. The following series of sports values would go some way to supporting such ventures:

- Losing with Character
- Winning with Character
- Playing Fairly
- Learning to be a Leader
- Coping with Pressure
- Being Disciplined
- Working as a Team
- Strengthening Your Weak Areas

The style of each sports value is to give plenty of opportunity for the children/young people to contribute to the discussion as seen by the following extract:

Losing with Character

Whatever our ability or position in life, we will all encounter losing at different stages. It may be a game, a race, a job or a relationship. For you to lose means that someone else has been able to win, and how we deal with this situation will tell us a lot about the progress we are making in life. To be tested in this way can help refine and polish your character. A good illustration is the one of the oyster that is irritated by the sand but uses this scratching to develop a beautiful pearl. Many people would have said that David Beckham was a loser when he was sent off in the 1998 World Cup game against Argentina because it appeared to lose the game for England. Despite all the criticism and obvious irritation from the media, he maintained his character and came through to captain his country for over fifty games after that.

Think

How do you think David Beckham felt after he received all the criticism for being sent off in such an important game?

What do you imagine he said to himself about his future?

The Bible is full of illustrations indicating how special we are in God's eyes, a fact that doesn't depend on whether we have lost or won. Jason Robinson captained the England rugby team and scored an important try in the final of the World Cup in 2003. His prayer before any game was not that his team might win but rather that he would play his very best and honour God by his attitude to opponents and officials alike.

Think

If you play the best you can and still lose, do you get discouraged?

What good things come out of losing when you have done your very best?

To lose with character is to be able to congratulate those who have won. Such an action may well be remembered by the winners long after they have forgotten the score. In many ways, learning how to lose is probably the best preparation for winning that you can think of. It makes you value your achievement at the same time as realizing what it is like to be on the losing side.

Think

Some people are so desperate to win that they will go to any lengths. What tricks do they get up to in order to bring this about?

How do these people lose by winning? What did Jesus mean when he said that 'the first shall be last and the last shall be first'?

Conclusion

There has never before been a time when so many sports ministry resources are available to the local church. Those detailed in this chapter are only the tip of the iceberg. Chapter 8 'Sports Ministries at Home and Abroad' will point you to many more and give you the necessary contact details. As for sports camps and Higher Sports, visit www.christiansinsport.org.uk and www.highersports.org to find out more information.

7

SECOND HALF PERFORMANCE

You do not stop playing when you grow old. You grow old when you stop playing

Anon

When churches are first approached about sport and recreation ministry, their thoughts are usually centred on either the young people's work or the possibility of a church football team. The prospect of an all-year-round programme with adults is generally far from their minds, with little or no consideration given to those in the 'second half' of their lives. It is in fact this group of senior adults, sometimes called the active retired, who are anxious to keep up their fitness levels and are on the lookout for new challenges in their lives. The market place has recognized the buying power of this ever-increasing group of people but as yet the church does not seem to have appreciated the influence they can have for the Kingdom of God.

The Office for National Statistics produced the 2001 Census, which revealed that the United Kingdom had more people over the age of 60 than under the age of 16, and that one million of its fifty-eight million inhabitants were over 85! By 2020, one third of the population in the UK will be over 50, with the majority expected to live for a further two or three decades after passing the Big Five-O. If the first twenty-five years of our lives can be described as 'preparation' and the next twenty-five as 'occupation', then there is no reason why the 50 to 75 years bracket can't be seen as 'transformation'. Unmissable Ltd, a company which has set out to offer its clients the chance to make their dreams come true, carried out a survey of a representative sample of 500 people in Britain. The survey discovered that the ages at which people make lists of the things they dream of doing in their lives proved to be the very young and the seriously mature. As people grew up, the survey results concluded, the wish list went away, but as the second half of life arrived, it was revised, updated and finally used as an agenda for the rest of life.

Boomer Generation

This boomer senior adult group that is now in the ascendant, grew up in a world of leisure, whereas their parents led harder lives which were work orientated throughout. The younger group views leisure as an expectation, not a reward. They have more time to plan for early retirement by saying 'What will I do?' rather than seeing it as a date to aim for and then giving everything up. Time and money will be spent on quality things and experiences.

However, this boomer generation is also an unseeded generation. Largely, they have not been brought up on Christian principles and don't know their Bible. Their desires lie in a number of directions:

- They are looking for a variety of experiences.
- They want to feel that they are being useful.
- They want to try new things.
- They are seeking a younger self-image.
- They like the personal touch in services and comfortable surroundings.

- They are planning for an expanded health span rather than merely a life span. Lifestyle and medical care serve to help this along.
- They are prepared to give serious time to good causes.

Growing Old Slowly

Dr Ken Cooper's philosophy is that 'it is better to grow old than to get old' (*Faith-Based Fitness*, 1997). Ageing is inevitable, but it is not inevitable that we do it at an accelerated rate. Average life expectancy in the UK now exceeds 75, yet many who come into that category are not really living, they are often just existing. Chronic health conditions have deprived them of their independence and self-control. A study on independence and ageing published in the US Public Health Services Prevention Report in October 1991 served to illustrate the enormity of this problem. The investigation revealed that in 1980, when life expectancy in the United States was nearly 74 years of age, the expectancy for a healthy life was only 62 years. In other words, Americans lived nearly twelve years of their life expectancy with some sort of chronic condition e.g. heart problem, joint disease or back ailment. These conditions were seriously affecting their quality of life. Cooper goes on to surmise:

But such a depressing result isn't inevitable. Our goal as we grow older should be, as gerontologists say, 'to square off the curve'. What this means is that as you age, bodily functions can be plotted on a linear graph with the curve dipping downwards from maximum health and capacity in the younger years to a cessation of functioning at death. For most people, there is a steady decline in physical functioning – a gradual dipping curve on the graph – which in effect leads to slow death in the last twelve years of life. But those who enter the advanced years in a healthy, fit state can actually condense the time of senility or limited capacity to function into a short period immediately prior to death.

My own father, Alf, continued his fitness regime into his 90s and had been working out in the gymnasium only six weeks before his death. Ken Cooper himself is now well into his 70s and maintaining a very high fitness level. His Dallas Clinic in Preventative Medicine continues to thrive.

Benefits of Fitness

There can be no doubt that fitness for those over 50 can have enormous benefits:

- A greater sense of fulfilment and well-being.
- Improved energy levels.
- Ability to focus on family activity and togetherness.
- Being a more active parent and grandparent.
- Less time spent in the doctor's surgery or the hospital ward.
- Freedom to help your relatives with their lives rather than them worrying about you.

Unfortunately, for many the picture is quite different. They are overweight, bulky around the middle and wouldn't contemplate breaking into a short run to save their lives. Any extended physical activity only aggravates muscles that have long been dormant, and leg muscles quickly start to cramp when there is a need to hurry for a late appointment.

The gap between wishing you were fit and getting fit seems insurmountable to so many. What they need is a ready-made programme that will cater for both their physical and their spiritual needs.

Where the Church Comes In

We must first face the fact that this 'second half' age group is one for which the church, so far, has no developed strategy. It is a group with high expectations, looking for changes in lifestyle and carrying a lot of experience. The local church will inevitably have such a group within its walls and an even larger group outside. In meeting the leisure and recreational needs of this group, the church will impact its community for Christ in a big way.

'Senior powerhouses' box below their chronological age

The New Breed

For those in the second half of life, new titles are often being bandied about. 'Grey power' came to the fore in 2002 when several football managers in their sixties found themselves in charge of successful Premier League clubs. Not for them a quiet desk job away from all the action. 'Senior powerhouses' are those who manage to retain the power of youth into their old age – they box below their chronological age. In recent years, Everett Hosack picked up gold medals in the 60 metres, 200 metres, the shot, throwing the weight and the super weight in the United States Masters Indoor Championships at Boston. He was 98 and competed for the Over the Hill Track Club! Hosack had retired from competitive sports in the 1920s but took it up again when he was 77. When asked if his daily garlic and multivitamin pills were the secret to long life, he replied that it was too early to tell because he had only been taking them since he was 95!

Harry Meistrup from Denmark was the world's oldest tennis player at 101. He played each week against his 87-year-old wife for two hours with no rest in between games. Noel Johnson from San Diego took up sport when he was 70, forty pounds overweight and had been given six months to live. At 88, he set a world age best for the marathon and ran, cycled and lifted weights until his death at 96.

Aristotle's proclamation that 'life is motion' would doubtless elicit a response from this new breed that 'motion is life'.

'Second Half' Recreation Programme

There is no reason why a sports ministry can't embrace and develop this group within an all-year-round programme. There will, of course, be programming implications peculiar to these folk that need careful consideration:

- They will respond to new challenges.
- They want to be fit and healthy.
- They are looking for meaning and purpose in life.
- They will have within their ranks tremendous and varied giftings that can help to expand sports ministry.
- They will be reliable and regular.

- They will be financially independent and supportive where expenses are required for kit, facilities, etc.
- They will have a strong network of close friends.
- They will vary from 'stay-at-homers' to those who want the ultimate challenge.

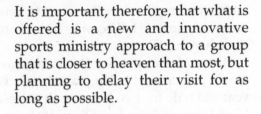

A group that is closer to heaven than most, but planning to delay their visit for as long as possible

It is important, therefore, that what is offered is a new and innovative sports ministry approach to a group that is closer to heaven than most, but planning to delay their visit for as long as possible.

Scope of the programme

'Retired' is not a biblical term and has no place in the life of a Christian. 'Redirected' is a worthy substitute, as demonstrated in the life of Caleb who, at the age of 85, asked God to 'give me this hill country' (Joshua 14:12). With this challenge ringing in our ears, let's look at the varied programme a church can offer in serving this 'transformation' age group.

- *Competitive team sports*: whatever the level of fitness, the muscles at this age take longer to recover from sustained activity and don't deal as well with quick movements as they used to do. The danger is for your mind to arrange an appointment that your body can't keep! We all like to think that we move at the speed of former years and are capable of doing the same tricks. For all these reasons, a lot of care needs to be taken over involving second-half folk in competitive team sports. There will usually be a 'Stanley Matthews type' – played top level league football at 50 – who belies his age and can hold his place with those who are twenty years his junior but, by and large, any regular activity involving the majority from this grouping should be of a modified fashion, e.g. senior five-a-side football on a small pitch, touch rugby, crown green bowls, short mat bowls, table tennis and cricket. Cricket is a particularly good competitive sport for playing well into your sixties. I write from experience!

- *Competitive individual sports*: this area offers a wide range of possibilities such as swimming, tennis and golf. Tournament ladders and ongoing competitions will be attractive to some. Pairings can be by age group or ability. Golf is a particular favourite, and some churches may see value in encouraging a number of 'second halfers' to take the game up and involve their friends at the same time. As a sport, it comes high on the list of friendship evangelism strategy.
- *Recreational sports*: these would be seen more in a social context and could be by team or individual. They would involve a lot of the activities named above but without the edge of sharp competition. Table games such as snooker, billiards, pool and table tennis fit into this category, as does tenpin bowling.
- *Wilderness/outdoor activities*: a whole variety of activities present themselves in this section. Hiking, walking, backpacking, camping, fishing, sailing, canoeing and skiing are ones that come to mind. Rambling weekends and walking retreats can be occasions when deep relationships are formed and the Christian life is actively role modelled.
- *Health and fitness*: this is possibly the area that interests second-half folk the most. Any church running its own health and fitness programme would have no difficulty recruiting this age group from inside and outside its

precinct. Because it is such a key area, I shall endeavour to expand my thinking regarding its implications.

There are basically three components to be considered for a complete conditioning programme:

1. endurance exercise (cardiovascular/aerobic)
2. strength work
3. stretching activities

With age, there is a natural deterioration of muscles and bones, as well as the inevitable loss of aerobic and cardiovascular power. With 10 per cent loss of muscle mass every decade after reaching 50 there is a real need to combat these areas of attrition.

Just do it

For many years, Anne Glover ran an aerobics/fitness programme at her church, Stafford Evangelical, for those over 60 and in their seventies and eighties. Her midweek session in the church hall also included lunch, creative activities and Alpha courses. Many unchurched folk have attended these over the years and have become assimilated into the life of the fellowship as a consequence. Church holidays and weekends away regularly included those from the fitness group, and one year the holiday on the south coast of England carried an Olympic theme for the week!

Endurance exercise

The medical recommendation of 20–30 minutes aerobic activity three times a week is a good guide for cardiovascular fitness. Brisk walking, jogging, cycling and swimming are the key activities here and should get the participant into the breathless zone with some sustained effort. Many find a regular regime of aerobic exercise difficult to maintain on their own and would welcome a weekly church activity that served this purpose. The devotional part of the activity could be planned to suit the group that is being served. To then encourage all members of the group to start their day with a 30-minute brisk walk would be an added bonus to their conditioning programme. Some individuals could also build up their friendship patterns by enrolling at the local fitness and health club. Such clubs are very conscious of this age group's desire to maintain good health patterns and have designer programmes to suit all levels of fitness.

Strength work

If the church is to run its own fitness programme, then a qualified instructor would be the first essential. Next to check on is the insurance cover for such activities in the church facility or hired premises. Training an instructor for this ministry is money well spent.

Training an instructor for this ministry is money well spent

Strength exercises can be better performed on weight machines in the local leisure centre – two 20-minute sessions per week would be ideal. However, a strength circuit can easily be devised in your church hall to include the following:

- sit ups (fingers touch tops of bent knees)
- squats (keep heels on ground and back straight)
- press ups (straight body and nose close to ground with each dip)

- biceps curls (hand weights or bags of sugar)
- triceps push-ups (hands behind you and on a bench – push up from there).

All these can be performed without equipment, apart from biceps curls, which need small hand weights. Individuals can then be encouraged to follow their own daily routine. A hand weights set can easily be purchased at the local sport shop in whatever weight is required.

Stretching activities

These are pretty vital if you are to prevent future back and joint complaints. Any church fitness activity should always start with a gentle warm up and end with a warm down of stretching activities. Present physical educationalists have differing views regarding warm ups but I always feel that

As you get older, it makes sense to concentrate even more heavily on a strength programme

the more you can inform your body that a change of pattern is coming, then the better it will react to the session. Any fitness book on your local bookseller's shelves will give you a range of stretching exercises you can do from your neck to your toes. Observing how a cat stretches is a good guide for starting your day as you stretch your body lying on the ground by reaching to the extremities with your hands and your feet. Then pushing your back gently into the floor will help to drain away any tension. Turning onto your front and

doing the superman exercise will do wonders for your lower back, i.e. as you lift your right arm then lift your left leg at the same time; reverse the procedure with left arm and right leg. Ten repetitions of each at a steady pace would be a good daily exercise for the back. If you are feeling on top form then try both arms and legs at the same time!

As you get older, it makes sense to concentrate even more heavily on a strength programme. Half your fitness time should be spent on exercises that will build up your muscles and bones, since your vulnerability to the loss of these tissues becomes a looming threat as your years advance. Small weights with low repetitions are always a good place to start and any fitness centre will help you devise an appropriate programme.

Temple of the Holy Spirit

The Apostle Paul makes reference to the body as the 'temple of the Holy Spirit' (1 Corinthians 6:19) and the 'temple of the living God' (2 Corinthians 6:16). He was aware of the need for the church to preach good stewardship of the body as well as of finances and time. A sport and recreation ministry with folk in the second half of their lives reaches deep into this concept and should be married with the spiritual journey that is in progress.

Two spiritual notables, John Wesley and C.S. Lewis, were only too well aware of this necessary balance all men and women require in their lives. Wesley's four-point plan was recorded in his journal for his eighty-fifth year as the reason why he had enjoyed such a long and energetic life:

1. Safeguard your daily devotion to God and make it part of your lifestyle.
2. Exercise regularly and seek a change of air.
3. Keep regular sleeping hours.
4. Be effective in managing stress.

C.S. Lewis, Christian writer and Oxbridge don, was a great walker who enjoyed sharing his walks with others and carrying out stimulating conversations with them. This is a great lesson to us all because one of the best motivations for keeping going on an exercise programme is to find a companion whose company you enjoy and who makes you look forward to each session. If this person is one who does not yet know Christ, then this can be an even greater motivation to maintain healthy exercise.

Walk and Don't be Faint (Isaiah 40:31)

The greatest and most achievable activity for the individual in the second half of life is undoubtedly that of walking. It is quietly becoming the most popular form of exercise in the UK and USA, with fitness experts and doctors recommending it more than any other form of exercise. It lowers the risk of heart attack, stroke, high blood pressure and a whole host of other preventable diseases. It is an exercise that can be done on your own, with a companion or in a large group; and one that is always worth the effort. For the one who is doubtful about starting a walking programme, the reminder of an old Chinese proverb is challenging – 'a journey of a thousand miles begins with a single footstep'.

Jesus was a great walker and fulfilled much of his ministry on the move. He taught his companions through stories and actions, often stopping to encourage, heal and teach many along the way. With his core team, he was able to section off quality time as they spent hours together on the dusty roads. Many of those conversations were so significant to the hearers that we have them recorded for our benefit in the gospels. Walking still allows opportunities for sharing our lives, just as it did all those years ago in Palestine.

Walking has a high profile in the whole of the Scriptures. The Hebrew word for walk, *halak*, occurs more than 1,500 times in the Old Testament, and there are countless recordings of the Greek word for walk, *peripateo*, in the New Testament. Both words mean much more than the act of physical movement, rather alluding to an individual's lifestyle or spiritual journey.

Walking has a high profile in the whole of the Scriptures

Walking offers opportunities for prayer that are not so easy with other physical exercises. An individual can go through his prayer list as he steps it out; two people can share and then pray for one another as they wander through the countryside; a whole church group can prayer walk in their neighbourhood by praying for the occupants of each house as they pass by.

Why walk?

Most healthy people can significantly improve their cardiovascular fitness in just twelve weeks with a thoughtful objective-based walking programme. Three objectives should be basic to any scheme:

1. An increase in your overall distance.
2. An increase in the amount of time spent walking.
3. An increase in the speed you walk at.

Walking is so effective at burning calories that it can actually produce weight loss with no dieting at all. Walking a mile at a brisk pace burns up around a hundred calories, a similar rate per mile to jogging. A slower pace does not mean less benefit; only that it takes a bit longer to chalk up the calorie total.

Walking can be so easily achieved and is more acceptable to millions who would have no interest in more strenuous activities. The drop-out rate as a consequence is negligible, especially when compared to the number that join gyms at the start of every New Year but rarely make it to March.

Dr Ken Cooper has highlighted four key times of the day for exercise: early morning, lunch, before evening meal, and at least one and a half hours after the evening meal. He recommends the early morning time for the reason that walkers are more likely to stick to their exercise habit because they are not faced with having to postpone it when unexpected events occur during the day.

Brisk walking

Where fitness is the primary goal, brisk walking rather than strolling is the recommended activity. The speed range runs from around 12–20 minutes per mile – three to five miles every hour. The slow end of this schedule produces many health benefits, and the fast end produces a significant aerobic workout. Most healthy walkers should be able to operate at the pace of 13–15 minutes every mile, which would get their heart well into the target zone for fat burning and cardiovascular improvement.

Good upright posture, straight legs and a bent arm swing are the necessary ingredients for stride lengthening and speed increase. A stronger pumping action with the arms and a greater drive with the legs will raise the heart rate and improve the time.

Finally, any exercise regime will be more effective if walking is supplemented with strength training. More muscle results in a greater calorie burn even when you are resting. This is because muscle is more metabolically active and adding two pounds of muscle weight will result in around

120–140 calories being burnt every day. For suitable strength exercises, refer back to the earlier section in this chapter on 'strength work'.

Nordic walking

This is ideal for combining endurance with both cardiovascular workout and strength improvement. It involves walking with specially designed poles, similar to ski poles, and is an all-year-round activity suitable for any weather and terrain. It evolved from off-season ski-training activity known as ski-walking, hill bounding or ski-striding, to become a way of exercising with poles all year round. Hikers with knee pain discovered that they could walk more powerfully with a pair of trekking poles, often eliminate or reduce hip, knee and foot pain, whilst backpackers found walking with poles can aid balance and facilitate walking. Although fitness walking with poles has been relatively slow to be embraced in North America, the Nordic-skiing savvy Northern Europeans quickly embraced this dry land hybrid of two of their favourite fitness activities: Nordic skiing and walking. A little more than a decade after its introduction into Europe, an estimated 8–10 million people have taken up fitness walking with specially designed poles as a regular form of exercise.

Nordic walking combines simplicity and accessibility of walking with simultaneous core and upper body conditioning, similar to Nordic skiing. The result is a full-body walking workout that can burn significantly more calories without a change in perceived exertion or having to walk faster. This is due to the incorporation of many large core and other upper-body muscles which comprise more than 90 per cent of the body's total muscle mass and do resistance work with each stride. Normal walking utilizes only 70 per cent of muscle mass with full impact on the joints of the legs and feet.

Nordic walking produces up to 46 per cent increase in energy consumption compared to walking without poles. It can also increase upper-body muscle endurance by 38 per cent in just twelve weeks.

Health benefits of Nordic walking

Compared to regular walking, Nordic walking involves applying force to the poles with each stride. Nordic walkers use more of their entire body with a greater intensity, and receive fitness building stimulation for the chest, laterals, triceps, biceps, shoulders, abdominals, spinal and other core muscles. The extra muscle involvement leads to enhancements over walking at equal paces in the following ways:

- Increased overall strength and endurance in the core muscles and the entire upper body.
- Significant increase in heart rate at the given pace.
- Greater ease in climbing hills.
- Burning more calories than in plain walking.
- Improved balance and stability with the use of poles.
- Significant unweighting of hip, knee and ankle joints (depending on the style used).
- Density preserving stress to bones of the upper and mid body.
- Increased stride length and walking speed.

To enter the 'second half' of life is a challenging occasion. If a sport and recreation programme can refresh and renew this age group in both body and spirit, then it will be responsible for lives that are richer, fuller and more in tune with the God of the Universe. The prophet Jeremiah reminded his readers of this great quest when he recorded these visionary words: 'ask where the good way is, and *walk* in it' (Jeremiah 6:16).

8

SPORTS MINISTRIES AT HOME AND ABROAD

The Bible talks about beginning close at home, then serving the wider region, and ultimately looking to needs around the world

Lloyd Reeb

Sports Ministries UK

Currently in the UK there exists an association of sports ministries which those involved have called SMUK – Sports Ministries UK. It is not an organization, does not have a constitution or membership, but has emerged as a twice-yearly meeting of leaders of Christian sports-related ministries which share a common concern for Christian work in the world of sport. Each represents a different niche, a distinct form of ministry. Each has a concern for contributing to the growth of God's Kingdom. Some are well established, some are newer and emerging. Some are widely known, some far less so. Some are operating nationally, some more regionally, but each is much more than a local church sports ministry. All are seeking to serve God and the wider church through their work, and each has a more than local church focus. SMUK is not a place for the leaders of the local church football team to meet with other local church equivalents from across the UK. Rather, it is for those ministries with a wider call, with national or at least multi-regional vision. The growth story of SMUK is an encouraging one.

Early Days

If we think of 'sports ministry' in the UK, most people might reflect on the role of Christians in Sport, which owes its origins to the call and vision of a quiet, unassuming, servant-hearted American, Eddie Waxer, who had seen in the USA how the Christian gospel could be communicated through sport, and who has shared that vision with the world over many decades! In the USA, Eddie had seen the rise of a multiplicity of 'sports ministries' and hoped that a pattern could be established around the world where sports ministry might emerge, without rivalry, as one ministry. He had made several trips to England to meet with Christians working in the sports world, as well as with Christian business people and, in 1976, took a group from the UK to a sports ministry conference in the USA to expose them to his vision. Among those were some of the early pioneers of UK sports ministry: a cricketing curate called Andrew Wingfield Digby; a tennis commentator, Gerald Williams; an ex-professional footballer who ran the Spurs shop, Harry Hughes; an Anglican vicar who had played Rugby Union for Sale, Alan Godson; a Baptist minister from Farnborough who was chaplain at Aldershot FC, Mike Pusey, and others. On their return they agreed to spread the vision of mission through sports ministry, and Christians in Sport was conceived!

Emergence of Christians in Sport

In the autumn of 1977, partly through Mike Pusey, partly through Alan West (then a player at Luton Town FC and a Christian) and partly through the openness of Graham Taylor, the then Manager of Watford FC, an official chaplaincy work started at the club. As a consequence of this development, the Watford chaplain, John Boyers, got to know of chaplains at Leeds United FC (John Jackson) and Stockport County FC (Jack Bingham). A network was in the making.

Andrew Wingfield Digby became involved in organizing a vision-sharing outreach dinner, funded by American support, in June 1978 at the Park Lane Hotel, London, at which he interviewed several UK sports-involved Christians and introduced Roscoe Tanner who was about to play at Wimbledon. From that dinner and the interest shown there, London Christians in Sport came about and Christians in Sport, generally, was strengthened.

Andrew began to give more of his time to this mission, with people like Tony Porter (now Bishop of Sherwood), Alan West, John Boyers, Alan Godson and Gerald Williams serving on a steering group. Christians in Sport then became a registered charity and more formal organizational steps followed.

In the late 1970s and 80s, these pioneers were sharing the vision of sports ministry in different ways, and seeds were being planted. Stuart Weir, now with Verité Sport, got involved as a volunteer and then as an employee of Christians in Sport; Graham Daniels, now General Director of Christians in Sport, came on board as a football ministry worker; Stuart and Andrew became co-directors, as advised by a review, to streamline management and decision making. With funding from the Deo Gloria Trust, Christians in

Sport grew considerably in size, influence and strength. But God was working in other ways, too.

New Shoots

At the beginning of the 1990s, Ambassadors in Sport and SCORE were set up in the UK, with Christians in Sport's blessing, and other seeds of sports ministry planted elsewhere were also beginning to emerge. The concept of Christians in Sport as an umbrella, sheltering and controlling sports ministry development in the UK, was no longer valid, since by the year 2000 the UK had several established and emerging sports ministries.

Because of the pace and variety of these ministry developments, some of the leaders were concerned about fragmentation and, in early 2003, Keith Hammond of Christians in Football, Dave Oakley of Ambassadors in Sport and John Boyers of SCORE talked and prayed about getting all leaders of known UK sports ministries together to talk about the nature of their respective work, and to consider how they might relate to each other more helpfully in the future. John Boyers was now chaplain at Manchester United FC, and Old Trafford was the setting for what can now be seen as the inaugural meeting of Sports Ministries UK.

International Partnership

In the autumn of 2003, the ISC (International Sports Coalition) held a major conference in Athens and introduced the concept of international mini regions for the purpose of linking together nations and sports ministries. Hermann Guehring, a German Christian, had seen the benefits of international co-operation in ministry within Europe through the European Christian Sports Union (ECSU) and saw here a template for world co-operation. This proposed structure was confirming that there should be linkage between sports ministries across the British Isles.

So from 2004 onwards, the UK sports ministry leaders' days have continued with a new impetus, leading to a greater trust and co-operation through mutual support and understanding of each ministry's progress and calling. Present meetings are now focusing on a combined strategy for the London 2012 Olympics in partnership with More Than Gold (see full details of MTG in Chapter 11).

The following pages give brief overviews of some of these national ministries as they seek to serve the wider church in the world of sport and recreation, as well as a glance at some international ministries that have also been significant in this area.

www.uksportsministries.org

AMBASSADORS IN SPORT (AIS)

Within the UK and across the world there are vast numbers of marginalized youngsters, vulnerable children and broken and hurt people that the church finds difficult to reach by conventional methods. Without the active support from people they trust and a focus that helps them think differently about themselves, the vulnerable and marginalized are very likely to continue in self-destructive behaviour patterns. However, through football, AIS workers are successfully able to come alongside broken and hurting people in a non-judgemental way so they can start to face issues and begin to deal with them in a way that enables life-changing decisions to be made.

The background to AIS is that in August 1990, three overseas amateur footballers, having relocated to the northern England town of Bolton, decided to start a football team by placing an advert in a local newspaper. From these humble beginnings a movement started that is Ambassadors in Sport, which has grown not only nationally across the UK but in many other countries around the globe. The ambitions of these founders of Ambassadors in Sport have always extended beyond the field itself; their Christian faith, ethos and values drove them to go beyond the game and actually seek to *'bring hope through football . . . one kick at a time'*.

Since becoming a UK registered charity and a limited company in 1997, Ambassadors in Sport has aspired to make a difference through:

1. Communicating the good news of Jesus

AIS seeks to visually and verbally demonstrate the gospel through appropriate methods to all people who engage with or participate in the football culture, specifically the poor, marginalized and the vulnerable, with a particular focus on children and young people. Examples of this activity include the following:

* Church-based community football outreaches through AIS teams.
* Two- to five-day soccer schools for 6- to14-year-olds.
* Schools work.
* Prison missions and youth offender programmes.
* Late evening leagues for inner-city gangs.

- Delivering life skills experience activities through football for homeless, unemployed and addicts.
- Overseas outreach through playing and coaching tours.

2. Encouraging and supporting churches to bring transformation to individuals and communities

As an organization, AIS seeks to be the facilitator of change within football culture and amongst people by providing football mission training for local churches. This is done by providing local, national and international initiatives through football ministry envisioning events, coaching courses, player programmes, internships, mentoring schemes, support networks and web-based resources.

www.ais-uk.org

CHRISTIANS IN SPORT (CIS)

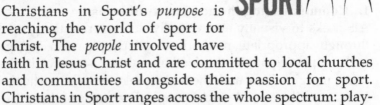

Christians in Sport's *purpose* is reaching the world of sport for Christ. The *people* involved have faith in Jesus Christ and are committed to local churches and communities alongside their passion for sport. Christians in Sport ranges across the whole spectrum: players, coaches, physiotherapists and match officials, young and old, amateur and elite, throughout the UK.

The first practical step for many who get involved in Christians in Sport is training to see how faith and sport connect; indeed that part of the sportsperson's worship of God can be their sport (that's right – their sport!). The next step of the journey is to realize that, as sportspeople, God has a specific mission for our lives: to help other sportspeople in the community hear the good news of Jesus and join the local church. Christians in Sport wants to encourage the instinctive *passions* that sport does matter to God; that God's word, the Bible, is relevant to sportspeople today and that telling teammates about the gospel is important.

Their *plan* for reaching the world of sport for Christ is pretty unsophisticated! They want to train each other to represent Christ in sports clubs, and to provide evangelistic speakers who know how to explain the Christian message to sporting friends in an appropriately accurate and winsome manner.

Try to imagine it: you're nervous as you start at a new club but you've tried to remember to pray for God to give you some good friends on the team. Tentatively, over the first couple of weeks, you mention to some of the team that you're a Christian and, inevitably, you get a mixed response; some are curious, for some it gives them ammunition for banter whilst some are a bit frosty – but you keep praying and trying to play on and off the pitch in a way that's honouring to God. You know that later on in the season your church is putting on a Christians in Sport multimedia sports quiz. So, when opportunities arise, you say something about the good news of Jesus and then nervously you invite your teammates to the quiz. To your surprise (isn't it always surprising!) four of them come along and have a great time. They go away having heard a talk that's fitting for the sports culture and clearly explains who Jesus is and why he lived and died. Now you're excited and you're starting to get what being a Christian in Sport is all about! You are reaching the world of sport for Christ.

This illustration is just a snapshot of what's happening currently all over the UK and what Christians in Sport hopes to see increasingly in each and every sports club in the country through young people, players in university clubs, adult teams and amongst professional and elite sports people.

Pray, Play, Say

When Fabio Capello took charge of the England football team, he said that part of his approach to improving their results was that 'players need to develop higher skill levels in all the core areas'. It sounds almost too simple, but as a manager who has pretty much won everything in the domestic and European game with professional clubs, to say this means we should probably sit up and listen. He's saying that players need to do brilliantly well in the 'core areas'.

One of the recurring questions Christians face is how to reach an increasingly secular culture with the good news of Jesus. It's a problem that troubles church leaders and individuals alike, and perhaps nowhere is it felt so keenly as in the culture of sport. There are myriad answers out there, from detailed cultural analyses to different styles of church. However, perhaps it seems too simple to say 'get Christians doing the basics of the Christian life brilliantly well in the core areas'. Yet in the Bible there is a real emphasis on this.

At the end of the letter to the Colossians, the Apostle Paul is answering just this question – how should Christians live in a secular culture? He emphasizes three areas where the gospel of Jesus Christ will lead to transformed and distinctive lives: prayer, godly living and gospel proclamation – or to make it memorable – *pray, play, say*.

Pray

> Devote yourselves to prayer, being watchful and thankful. And pray for us, too, that God may open a door for our message, so that we may proclaim the mystery of Christ, for which I am in chains. (Colossians 4:2–3)

Our first recognition must be that engaging with and reaching into secular culture is beyond our capabilities. However, Christ is Lord over everything and that includes culture, so we need to commit to praying, asking him to work and to provide open doors for the gospel message.

Play

> Be wise in the way you act towards outsiders. (Colossians 4:5)

At the same time as praying, very often Christians living distinctive lives in the culture will provoke people to consider Jesus Christ. Our work, our rest, our play – our whole lives – are a vital consideration, particularly in an age when people want to not only see whether something is 'true' but also whether it works in practice.

Say

> Let your conversation be always full of grace, seasoned with salt, so that you may know how to answer everyone. (Colossians 4:6)

The Kingdom of God has always advanced through gospel proclamation and so it is important that Christians are equipped to tell others about Jesus' life, death and resurrection – this will be the 'saltly' content of our conversations. Alongside this, though, it needs to be spoken with grace, such that the message is backed up by the manner in which it is spoken.

So how do we reach the world of sport for Christ? Well, there may be lots of different methodologies and strategies that are worth considering, but sometimes we can over complicate something that is actually quite simple – stick with the fundamentals by trusting in Jesus and *pray, play, say.*

www.christiansinsport.org.uk

HIGHER SPORTS

Higher Sports began its life in 2005 as the result of a conversation between father and son, and a desire to equip the local church  with an attractive resource to reach its community for Christ through the medium of sport.

Bryan Mason, in his role as European Director for Church Sports and Recreation Ministers (CSRM), had always returned to the UK from his many USA visits inspired by the effectiveness of Upward Basketball, a church-based resource that was changing the lives of young people in the USA by its outstanding coaching techniques and vibrant Christian teaching. Deciding that the UK church was not yet ready for basketball, Bryan and Ben Mason founded Higher Sports Limited, with the first product being Higher Rugby, tag rugby for boys and girls.

Ben had played rugby at national league level and was a qualified grade three coach with the RFU. Bryan had worked for Christians in Sport for nine years as their National Co-ordinator for Church Sports Ministry. This combination meant that Ben wrote the coaching drills for the eight-session course and Bryan added the devotionals on the life of Daniel – 'Daniel, a First Team Player'.

This resource enabled churches to run the course over eight weeks, during a national or international rugby competition or as a sports clinic or holiday club. The pack came with all the coaching and teaching manuals, as well as the kit and equipment required. A particular feature was the 'powerball' – a coloured rugby ball that could be used for explaining about the Christian life. Tevita Vaikona, ex-Bradford Bulls RL, Saracens RFU and Tongan international, provided strong support to the project, and so Higher Rugby was up and running!

Three years later, John Squires of Ambassadors in Sport produced the coaching and teaching modules for Higher Football, and a number of churches were able to use this resource during the World Cup football competition in South Africa 2010. In the same year, Higher Sports became an approved Christian charity and began work on producing Higher Games, a resource tailor-made for churches wanting to make an impact in their communities during the London Olympics of 2012.

www.highersports.org

KICK LONDON

Kick London is a sports coaching charity which seeks to make 'a transformational difference to the lives of young people, through sport', by working in schools and with local churches across London, coaching various sports and using sport to introduce young people to Jesus. Many pupils have little or no contact with the gospel or the church. Kick London is a godly presence in schools, being 'salt and light'. By providing schools with a service they need, they earn the right to be there, the right to have a Christian presence on the sports field or in the gym.

It was an Ofsted inspector who said it is now schools, not churches, which are at the centre of the community. Whether you agree with this or not, there are great opportunities for Christians to engage with schools in creative and innovative ways. Kick London is one of those ways.

Their sports coaches deliver PE lessons, lunchtime/after school clubs and sessions in the holidays, as well as assemblies and mentoring; linking sports coaching with life skills and incorporating the statutory 'Social and Emotional Aspects of Learning' (SEAL) programme. In practice, Kick London coaches the skill of 'passing' and links this to 'sharing and relationships'. 'Shooting or scoring' skills are linked to 'ambition and going for (life) goals'. Weekly themes are related to Bible passages, but as they're in schools to coach sport, there are limited opportunities to share the gospel. However, the values are Bible based and all the coaches are Christians, who are good role models and take opportunities whenever opportunities arise. This could be a pupil asking 'Is God more important than your family?' or chatting with other adults in the staff room. They sow lots of seeds but find it hard to spend quality time with people in order to deepen relationships.

One way to build relationships, however, is by linking pupils from schools with local churches, using football academies. These are two-hour sessions at the weekend, run in partnership with churches near schools where Kick London is working. Open to the whole community, they provide a good opportunity to connect young people from schools with young people from church. Football is a great way to engage with people and get to know them. This is an opportunity to help churches to use sports ministry to reach out to local young people. They are helped to see sport as an outreach tool and a way of introducing young people to Jesus, helping them become part of a Christian community. At the academies, the football skill is linked with the life skill, and a theme from the Bible is introduced e.g. passing, making choices in life and walking in light or darkness.

Recently coaches ran the youth section of a tournament. Two boys from an academy made eternally significant decisions to follow Jesus during the gospel presentation. Seeing them respond was truly amazing. For those of us who do so much sowing into people's lives, seeing the fruit of our labour is so encouraging.

www.kicklondon.org.uk

KING'S FOUNDATION

The King's Foundation is a UK educational charity, dedicated to developing children through sport in the UK, Europe and the developing world. Established  in 1991, the King's Foundation aims to assist the physical, emotional and spiritual development of young people by providing them with support in delivering sporting, moral and spiritual principles and practices around the world, regardless of religion, race or ethnicity.

For nearly two decades, the King's Foundation has effectively used sport to benefit children and young people throughout the UK and Europe and, most recently, in Africa through development programmes and King's Camps International. The King's Foundation uses sporting activities together with biblically-based activities to develop children's physical, emotional and spiritual capabilities in the hope of them becoming responsible members of society and improving their condition of life.

Helping UK Families

For over nineteen years, the King's Foundation has provided subsidized child places on King's Camps (multi-activity holiday camps) for disadvantaged families in the UK. More recently the King's Foundations' Supporting Families programme has established links with local hospices, schools, social workers, foster care organizations and family support workers to ensure that those families most in need receive assistance.

Work in Africa

Since 2002, the King's Foundation has been working with disadvantaged communities in Botswana and Uganda with the primary purpose of developing individuals and organizations that work with children. They provide support by training and developing local volunteers in sports leadership in order to make a difference to the lives of children most in need. Their aim is to transform individuals and communities by developing sustainable programmes run by indigenous people, and they look to partner with individuals, churches and organizations that share their values.

The King's Foundation development programmes have already benefitted thousands of children in sub-Sahara Africa, and the hope is to reach out to more children by transferring proven programmes to other communities throughout the world.

The King's Foundation is committed to improving the quality of children's lives and is passionate about their development by providing support to families and sports programmes for children throughout the world. They donate their time, services and around 8 per cent of King's Camps' income to providing services to UK families in need, and to establishing similar organizations in developing countries. The income-generating work of the King's Foundation fully covers administrative and management costs, thus enabling all supporters' donations to go directly to development work.

The King's Foundation's shared philosophy: 'We get one go at life on earth, so work to make a difference, make the journey as enjoyable as possible, don't be constrained by tradition, take others on the journey.'

www.kingsfoundation.com

SCORE – SPORTS CHAPLAINCY SPECIALISTS

Serving Sport through Chaplaincy

The vision for SCORE came initially from leaders of the Baptist Union of Great Britain who, in 1990, advised one of their ministers to consider using his experience in sports chaplaincy in a full-time capacity for the benefit of the wider church. Thus SCORE was set up and gained registered charitable status in 1991, aiming to resource and develop high-quality chaplaincy to the sports world. It has grown remarkably since then – the administrative office now holds the details of around two hundred chaplains who belong to a variety of church backgrounds, and who SCORE seeks to support as they serve local sports clubs.

SCORE is essentially an envisioning, resourcing and networking agency. Virtually all of the sports chaplains it seeks to involve are ordained clergy. Thus they have training in pastoral theology, experience in pastoral ministry and the affirmation of their denominational headquarters as persons suitable for chaplaincy work. The chaplains, and the clubs, are asked to agree to the SCORE Code of Practice. Each chaplain gives one day per week or more to working with staff, players and associates of the local sports club. This is real ministry commitment, not a means of associating with a club or players! The chaplains make their pastoral and spiritual support available to whoever may need it, working with sensitivity in a non-confrontational way, and over a long period of time becoming trusted by the club and its employees.

SCORE chaplains work right across the UK in a variety of sports, employing a small paid staff, augmented by volunteers, who together oversee chaplaincy in various sports and different parts of the UK. SCORE also has a strong portfolio of major sports event chaplaincy, with experience in both organizing and delivering chaplaincy at Commonwealth, Olympic and Paralympic Games, and other world gatherings. Their work has received real affirmation and support from the highest levels of sports organizations, with the work in horse racing, Rugby League, Rugby Union and Association Football particularly prominent.

There is an annual three-day SCORE Sports Chaplaincy Conference which takes place in early October at the National Sports and Recreation Centre, Lilleshall, Shropshire, and is open to all existing and prospective chaplains. This gathering also incorporates the AGM of the charity.

SCORE can help local clergy who might be considering a sports chaplaincy involvement, or support their church activities by providing staff or club chaplains to speak at services, outreach meetings, breakfasts, etc. Help is also available to those in sports organization and administration by the provision of suitable and trained personnel to serve as chaplains, or by organizing chaplaincy programmes and training for sports events.

Most UK sports ministries recognize SCORE as the sports chaplaincy specialists, and they are trusted by sports bodies in the UK to deliver excellent chaplaincy provision.

www.sportschaplaincy.org.uk

SPIRIT IN SPORT

Spirit in Sport is a classic example of how one man's full-time ministry evolved from years of voluntary sports work that started within his own church youth group. Chris Cox worked tirelessly with adults and young people alike in developing a sports programme at St Jude's Church in Southsea, Hampshire, a church which gained national prominence as a beacon church through its ongoing relationship with Christians in Sport, and its outstanding sports ministry work in the community. As the work grew over the years, more and more non-church people were joining St Jude's regular sports events, which included swimming galas, various tournaments (badminton, netball, table tennis, rugby, tennis and football), as well as overseas football tours and keep-fit classes. All these activities culminated with the bringing together of all the winners and participants at an end-of-season sports breakfast. Here, trophies were awarded and a short talk given that was relevant to sport and the Christian faith.

Regularly meeting with non-Christian friends on neutral territory, and in non-threatening and familiar environments, has given Chris and his team strong links with the community. A yearly holiday sports camp has also served to develop positive relationships with many families and local schools.

Having wrestled with organizing this packed programme together with family commitments and holding down a full-time job, it became more and more obvious to Chris that this was what God was calling him to do full-time. However, leaving the security of a paid job of more than thirty years took a lot of courage and faith. He felt lacking in both, but thankfully God was patient and loving and kept giving him gentle nudges in the right direction.

In January 2010, he left full-time paid employment to head up the non-profit group Spirit in Sport, and is now able to network his community for Jesus through sport as never before. Chris is an inspiration to any man or woman who has a passion for both Jesus and sport and is ready to put themselves at God's disposal in this very privileged ministry. As Chris will testify, it is an exciting and challenging ride with thrilling results.

www.spiritinsport.co.uk

SPORTING 87

History

Sporting 87 Football Club was formed, as the name suggests, in 1987, to allow Christians to play football in an environment where they could share their faith with other local football teams in the community. Since the early days, the club has developed and progressed enormously and, recently, the club has been awarded FA Charter status for both adult and youth teams. The club has

a tradition of playing football in a correct manner, keeping to the laws of the game and remaining in good spirits throughout matches. The club welcomes both Christians and non-Christians who would enjoy being part of this set-up.

Adult teams

Currently, Sporting 87 has three adult teams. The First and Reserve teams play in the Suffolk and Ipswich League (SIL), whilst the Third team, Sporting A, play in the local St Edmundsbury Football League. For two nights a week, the adult teams are trained by a UEFA 'B' licensed coach.

Youth teams

Sporting 87 has ten youth teams, with around 160 youth players in age groups ranging from under 11s to under 16s. All Sporting 87 youth teams play on Saturday mornings in a league called South Suffolk Youth Football League (SSYFL). Youth players are encouraged to progress into the adult teams when they reach the age of 16, and there is training for each age group once a week with FA qualified coaches. All of the youth coaches are part of churches in the area, which maintains the Christian ethos throughout the teams.

Honours

The club has received many awards over the years, the most recent being the Suffolk FA Fairplay award. In the 2008/09 season, the Reserve squad gained promotion to SIL (Suffolk and Ipswich League) Division 4, with the First team finishing fourth in Division 2. The following season, the First team reached the final of the Snailwell Cup and won the National Christian Football Festival trophy in Manchester.

In 2009, Sporting 87 won the prestigious Suffolk FA Charter Club of the Year award.

Links

The club is interdenominational, with its players, coaches and supporters all having links with many different local churches. In addition, Sporting 87 has a number of very strong links and associations with local, national and international Christian organizations. Each year the club sends some members of its youth teams to the USA to work with On Goal, a Christian football organization that runs summer camps. One of the players recently spent six months with On Goal Brazil, on a street soccer programme.

Mission statement

Sporting 87 is a Christian football club, dedicated to playing football to the highest possible standards of competition, ability and good conduct. The club is committed to developing the Christian growth of its members and being an ambassador for Christ to those it meets.

www.sporting87.co.uk

SPORTS FORCE

Sports Force is a great example of how an individual, passionate about sports ministry in the local church, can make such a difference in the community for Jesus Christ,

at the same time as becoming a 'sports force' in the nation.

Mark Blythe was a very keen amateur sportsman when, aged 35, God saved him. Having been in event management and played as many sports as possible but particularly football, cricket, golf, running and triathlons, it soon became clear that sports ministry was the specific calling on Mark's life. The first 35 years was just preparation for this!

God cleverly placed Mark in a church with a football team that has now grown to four adult teams playing each week and a free football group for fifty youngsters every Saturday morning. After fifteen years of running the football club, Mark has made every mistake possible and he is keen for others not to do the same! With this in mind he has written a book called *Football 2 Football Ministry 3* – away wins are hard to come by – which details, through all the struggles, how lives have been changed through vibrant football ministry.

A new golf ministry has been established within the church which stages five events a year, a weekend tour and weekly social games. The Church Cricket Club has won the National Christian Cup and has an annual weekend away, as well as playing social but competitive matches. Whichever sport or pastime church members are into, Mark encourages folk to see that as their mission field – it's easier to reach like-minded people.

Mark helped to establish, and now maintains, the website that lists all the sports ministry organizations that he has found so far in the UK. If you love Jesus and sport, then this is the place to look **www.uksportsministries.org**.

If a church is interested in starting or reviewing their sports ministry, then Mark would be a good person to talk to.

www.sportsforceinternational.org

2K PLUS INTERNATIONAL SPORTS MEDIA

2K Plus International Sports Media (2K Plus) is the world's only Christian sports media agency. It produces radio programmes and reports with a Christian perspective from major sporting events around the world. It also produces a weekly English language programme, *Planet Sport*, broadcast on thirty stations worldwide.

Mission statement

To promote a relevant, alternative, Christ-centred lifestyle to sports fans around the world.

Aims

2K Plus has two aims:

1. to challenge sports fans to become followers of Jesus Christ and members of his church worldwide
2. to strengthen the faith of those who already follow Jesus.

2K Plus has covered the past five summer Olympics, and London 2012 will be the sixth. In 1992 a small team produced radio reports and features from the Olympic Games in Barcelona, in English and Spanish, primarily for a missionary radio station in Quito, Ecuador. Such was the interest that demand for their services grew until, twelve years later, in 2004, a team of sixteen media professionals at the Olympic Games in Athens produced radio material in eight languages that was broadcast on over 1,000 radio stations. Four years later in Beijing, a team of fifteen produced programmes in seven languages that were heard on about 1,500 stations.

Programmes are carried mostly, but not exclusively, by Christian stations and networks. At the 2010 FIFA World Cup, 2K Plus interviews and features were also broadcast by BBC World Service (Africa), the national broadcaster ZBC in Zimbabwe, and local government station Paradise FM in Seychelles.

Churches

During the 2012 Olympics, 2K Plus will be offering many audio resources on their website for churches to use as a part of their own ministry. These are designed to meet the two aims stated above.

Sports fans

A range of resources will be available to offer sports fans outside the church. These will include a series of one-minute programmes in which Olympic athletes talk about one aspect of their sport and faith as a follower of Jesus Christ. These stand-alone programmes provide the opportunity to discuss sport and personal faith. Programmes can be downloaded and played during a service or other meetings, and sports fans can be directed to them on the website.

Programmes that are designed to attract and interest the sports fan will also be posted daily on the website www.2kplus.org.uk. These will include reports from the Games, interviews with athletes, including those who follow Jesus Christ, and news from the arts and cultural events in London during the Olympics.

To strengthen the faith of sports fans that already follow Jesus, 2K Plus provides several series of Devotional

Podcasts on the website and, during the Olympics, reports will be posted on the various Christian mission, service and outreach activities happening across the capital and country to inform and encourage the Christian public.

www.2kplus.org.uk

VERITÉ SPORT

Verité Sport is essentially the ministry of Stuart Weir, who was previously a director of Christians in Sport for fifteen years. Stuart has written extensively on the relationship between the Bible and sport. He is one of the few writers who try to engage the Bible with the mindset of the elite sportsperson. He writes at an academic level but seeks always to be down to earth and practical. His article 'Never on Sunday' on Sunday sport is a good example.

The Verité Sport website is a useful resource, in particular the download section which includes a great choice of material:

- Books like *What the Book Says About Sport* and *Born to Play* can be found in downloadable format and in several languages.
- Articles on sports ethics.
- Over two hundred short devotional reflections on sport.
- Book reviews – reviews of over a hundred books of relevance to sports ministry.
- A recommended ten best books to read on sports ministry.
- An extensive bibliography of materials on Bible and sport.

Church links

Stuart travels extensively overseas and has developed a number of sports projects seeking to help the local people in many helpful ways, at the same time as sharing the gospel. He would be delighted to link up with any church interested in playing a part in the ministry. For example:

- Ukraine – developing football coaches in churches by helping coaches improve their skills and qualifications. Verité Sport seeks to help them become more effective in their ministry.
- Togo – supporting a girls' football initiative by providing boots, balls and kit for the girls, as well as small grants to enable the club to cover the cost of taking part in the league.
- Congo – supporting a football coaching project for children, run by a former captain of the national team, by providing equipment.
- Pakistan – financial support for a cricket tournament to bring people together.

Blogger extraordinaire

Stuart's daily blogs from Beijing and Delhi have given a good insight into his unique ministry with Verité Sport. His press status, writing for the *Oxford Mail* and *Times Online*, gives him great opportunities to meet with key athletes and provide them with personal support and encouragement, whilst his linguistic skills enable him to carry out significant interviews with both athletes and spectators, an area where he works closely with 2K Plus.

www.veritesport.org

WORLD SPORT MINISTRIES

World Sport Ministries (WSM) was birthed in 1999 when God spoke to Grant Sheppard to begin a ministry that seeks to serve the local church and reach communities for Christ.

WSM's mission is to 'Reach the world for Jesus through sport'; its vision is to begin Community Sports Teams (CSTs) that prayerfully stage events and projects to impact people for Jesus through sport and leisure wherever God opens doors. A Community Sports Team is equipped for service and consists of sports-minded people from local churches within a community or city. This team is trained, equipped and empowered by WSM to add a sports ministry dimension to what churches are doing, and to stage events that enable them to reach out even more effectively into their area. Teams do vary in what they deliver, but current ministry includes schools coaching, discipleship groups, holiday sports camps, sports academies, Kids Games, sports dinners, quizzes, men's breakfasts, major sports event screenings and various community tournaments.

Kids Games has impacted the world over the last decade and this effective ministry of sports evangelism has spread to over a hundred countries with remarkable instances of local church growth in its wake. Opening and Closing Ceremonies and then content for ten days of activities and Christian teaching have seen millions of youngsters influenced by the good news of Jesus. WSM is committed to this exciting programme and has introduced it to the UK. It will be working with UK Sports Ministries to role model this outreach activity before, during and after the London Olympics, in co-operation with many churches throughout the land.

To date, WSM has started teams in Bath, Bristol and Newham within the United Kingdom, and is developing a growing ministry in Kenya. WSM has partnered with many churches and organizations nationally and internationally, including mission trips to ten other nations.

WSM has a heart to see believers working together in unity through outreach and has passion, experience and resources to establish sports ministry teams that really impact communities and that develop leaders through training and mentoring.

www.worldsportministries.com

YOUTH FOR CHRIST

Since 1999, Youth for Christ has been committed to the use of sport as a means of taking the good news of new life in Jesus to the young people of Britain in a way that is relevant to them.

Pioneered through the Fly basketball team in 1999, the work has continued to develop through Football and Skate by connecting with young people in their own environment.

Youth for Christ's itinerant sports mission team, Nomad, tours with a sports cage that can be used as a mobile venue for games (Panna KO) of two versus two players. In and around the cage, the YFC team is able to create an instant sporting arena which enables young people of all levels and skills to take part. Through the discussions, the team is able to address issues of faith and life with the watching crowd.

A street football pitch is utilized in Scotland along the same lines. Accompanied by the work in over two hundred schools, summer conferences and even the Alton Towers campus, well over 100,000 young people have been reached through this sports ministry.

Church engagement

Through school assemblies and lessons, YFC is exploring the use of healthy lifestyles and physical activity to help young people discover a positive attitude in their lives and the God who wants to be involved with them. The programmes introduced serve to challenge young people in their technical knowledge, social ability, physical fitness and spiritual awareness. Each day they are encouraged to do, think or say something that will help them pursue these areas of their life.

In some regions, YFC is looking to develop Global Community Games, in partnership with local churches, as an event to engage young people in the community in competitive sporting activity that has a strong emphasis on enjoyment and achievement. The West Midlands is leading the way with its regional approach to sports ministry development, particularly with the resource CRUX Sports. This specific sports ministry tool is used for coaching in schools across the curriculum. In many areas, churches are partnering with schools in this resource to make a real difference to young lives.

As Sports Ministry Advisor, Barry Mason represents YFC and the organization's interest in sports activity. He is the first port of call for anyone interested in working with YFC in any of these ventures.

FURTHER SPORTS MINISTRIES IN THE UK

Christians in Football
www.christiansinfootball.org

Christian Surfers UK
www.christiansurfers.co.uk

Lions Raw
www.lionsraw.org

Logos Golf Ministries
www.logosgolfministries.com

Operation Mobilisation Sports Link
www.omsportslink.org

Sporting Marvels
www.sportingmarvels.com

Sports Pursuits
www.sportspursuits.org

CHURCH SPORTS INTERNATIONAL

After having served the local church for twelve years, and having been part of a developing local church, national and international sports ministry, Rodger Oswald  felt led to found and direct Church Sports International (CSI) – a ministry devoted to serving the local church in order to create culturally relevant and strategic evangelism and discipleship through sports and recreation ministry.

In CSI's eighteen years of ministry, over seventy countries, hundreds of American churches and thousands of individuals have been served. That service was given through consulting, equipping and personal training through major events and conference/seminar efforts, as well as personal and single or multi-church training programmes. To augment this equipping, CSI created training resources – currently offering sixteen instructional manuals, twenty-seven hours of DVD and CD training, and a Learning by Extension (correspondence) programme. In addition, CSI has recruited and trained nineteen international associates in seventeen countries. These global partners have their own ministry, but also represent CSI and its commitment to the local church. One other contribution of CSI is through institutions of higher learning. Rodger has been instrumental in creating the first Sports Ministry major degree at a university and has helped another dozen institutions create their own Sports Ministry training curriculum.

In serving the US church, different responses have come to light. Some churches lack any sort of evangelistic fervour and, therefore, reject the notion of using sports as a means of reaching out to unbelievers. Other churches, while evangelistic, are not able to grasp the cultural relevance of sport and the fact that this conduit gives them the widest possible entry into the lives of the unsaved. They, too, see no need to employ sports and recreation ministry as part of an evangelistic strategy or church programme.

There were churches that struggled with sports ministry for biblical/theological reasons, and there were churches that struggled philosophically: 'How does this fit into the overall church ministry?' 'This was never taught at my Bible school.' 'Would Jesus compete?' 'Isn't sports worldly?' Once a biblical apologetic was supplied, some embraced sports ministry, but others did not.

The evangelistic churches, and those that grew in appreciation of the viability and value of sports ministry, began employing sporting and recreational activities as a means of bridging from the worship centre to the community of unbelievers. In some cases it was through on-going team competition (leagues), in other cases it was through individual competitive sports. Churches learned the degree to which people were involved recreationally and the church began to develop outdoor ministries (camping, hunting, fishing, backpacking), fitness ministries (aerobics, walking/jogging, flexibility and strength conditioning, weight management/control) and even leisure activities (sewing, quilting, board games).

The maturation of the phenomenon of sports ministry has given a vital evangelistic platform to the church. US churches are moving from major events such as the Super Bowl (American football championship) or national premierships, to communicating the gospel through numerous creative means (home meetings, big screen presentations, camps and instructional clinics, literature distribution). Not only has this phenomenon given a strong evangelistic platform, but it has created a tool by which the believer can be discipled in the faith. The fact is that US churches employing sports ministry wisely, have seen significant numerical and spiritual growth. The credo is 'We may be using a game, but we are not playing a game. Eternity is serious business.'

www.churchsports.org

CHURCH SPORTS AND RECREATION MINISTERS (CSRM)

CSRM has its roots in the last quarter of the twentieth century when thousands of American churches had built athletic facilities on their campus but struggled with the unique nature and challenge of sports outreach. Sports pastors found themselves isolated, outworked, under-appreciated and woefully under-resourced. A small group of these 'sports ministers' formed themselves into an organization for those planning to use sports as a ministry in the church and, in the mid-1990s, CSRM was officially incorporated.

Under the guidance of its Executive Director, Dr Greg Linville, and a gifted Board of Directors, CSRM is seeing the dream become a reality as it endeavours to 'equip local churches to change lives through sport'. This is achieved by means of a four-fold strategy based on a 'Four "C" Initiative' – Conference, Consulting, Certification and Connection, all of which are supported by the Core of staff and Board who serve to support these initiatives.

Conference

This takes the shape of an annual sports ministry summit with speakers and delegates from around the world as well as America. Regional and Specialist Conferences also take place from time to time. The annual conference is the driving force of CSRM and, arguably, the greatest exponent of church sports ministry teaching and practice across the nations.

Consulting

CSRM offers churches a sports ministry mentoring programme as well as a coaching-of-coaches programme.

Certification

A strong certification programme is backed up by teaching and continuing education.

Connection

In many large cities in the US there is a SOLD programme (Sports Outreach Leadership Development) which connects churches together for encouragement, training and support.

The underpinning core values of CSRM enable the organization to fulfil its mission statement:

www.csrm.org

SPORTS OUTREACH INTERNATIONAL

Sports Outreach International has developed over the years into a leadership training ministry that is keen to reproduce reproducers.

Their main purpose is evangelism and discipleship, which can take them into many areas of life. For over twenty years, SOI has been committed to getting behind young leaders and organizations to help them to succeed in being a healthy, dynamic ministry. SOI has been involved in helping train, resource and encourage people and their organizations to reach the universal people group – those that are interested in sport.

Why Sports Ministry

Sport and evangelism

On a communication level, sport can be used as an effective delivery mechanism for the gospel. Sport builds an amazing system for relationship-building and trust. This powerful connection of relationship creates an opening to encourage the heart with the gospel message.

Sport and discipleship

Again, the interaction of sports people is such a strong relational force that it can be a wonderful opportunity to convey, model and teach Christian living. Of course, the opposite is true too; sport can be a system to transmit all sorts of unhealthy habits and paradigms.

The power of sport

Sport and recreation play an important role at the individual, community, national and global level. For the individual, sport enhances one's personal abilities, general health and self-knowledge. On the national level, sport and physical education contribute to economic and social growth, improve public health, and bring different communities together. On the global level, if used consistently, sport and physical education can have a long-lasting positive impact on development, public health, peace and the environment.

Sport and education

Sport and physical education are an essential element of quality education and leadership development. They promote positive values and skills which have a quick but lasting impact on young people, as well as a tendency to permeate their immediate culture. Sports activities and physical education generally make school more attractive and improve attendance. The core values integral to sportsmanship make sport a valuable method of promoting peace, from the local to the international scale.

Sport and peace

Sport, as a universal language, can be a powerful vehicle to promote peace, tolerance and understanding. Through its power to bring people together across boundaries, cultures and religions, it can promote reconciliation. For example, sport has helped re-initiate dialogue when other channels were struggling: North and South Korea; table tennis set the stage for the resumption of diplomatic ties between China and the USA in 1971; and today, many other natural enemies like Israeli and Palestinian children regularly come together to play soccer or basketball.

Sport and health

Regular physical activity and play are essential for physical, mental, psychological and social development. Good habits start early: the important role of physical education is demonstrated by the fact that children who exercise are more likely to stay physically active as adults. Sport also plays a major positive role in one's emotional health, and allows you to build valuable social connections, often offering opportunities for play and self-expression.

www.sportsoutreach.com

SOLA (SPORTS OUTREACH LOS ANGELES)

Sports Outreach Los Angeles (SOLA) was founded in 1992 as the Los Angeles chapter of Sports Outreach America. SOLA was tasked with developing outreach programmes through local churches which would employ the excitement generated by major sporting events. The first outreach, co-ordinated around the 1994 Football World Cup (finals were in the Los Angeles area), included 300 churches. In the same year, an outreach surrounding the LA Marathon was launched and has continued every year since then. In 1995, SOLA began training church leaders in the ongoing use of sport and recreation activities apart from those scheduled around major events. Furthering this training development SOLA launched its Sports Outreach Leadership Development programme (SOLD) in 2000. Steve Quatro, Executive Director of SOLA, has taught sports ministry at Azuza Pacific University for the past five years and recently published a book outlining six principles for effective sports ministry – *Intentional Outreach*.

The Olympic Torch Relay provides a great way to reach out before all of the bright lights of the Olympic Games dim everything else.

As a result of SOLA's involvement in the LA Marathon, Steve was asked to serve on the Official Olympic Committee which was tasked with encouraging and organizing community celebrations along the Torch Relay Route.

SOLA prayerfully decided that the strategy for ministry along the Torch Relay Route would be to identify churches on or near the route, then encourage them to host celebratory events which would piggyback on the excitement of the

Torch Relay. The churches would then invite the community to participate in these events in order to build relationships with people outside their congregations.

SOLA co-hosted two events with local churches, in order to help these churches build relationships with their neighbours, with the ultimate goal of earning the privilege of sharing the gospel of Jesus Christ. While one event had limited impact, the other was considered by all of the ministries involved to be an effective outreach to unchurched members of the community.

One ministry site was at a downtown park, a few blocks from the sponsoring church. The church planned a music-themed event which featured musical groups made up of children and adults. From SOLA's perspective, this event was mildly successful because not many people, other than friends and family of the performers, came to see them perform. And furthermore, after the Torch went by (it was in front of the event for less than a minute) most of the people left. There was not sufficient time for relationship building.

The other event was sponsored by a church located a few hundred metres off the Route. This sports-themed event was held in a bank car park which was on the official Torch Relay Route. The bank allowed free use of the car park, their toilets inside the bank, and they also contributed financially while the church planned the entire event and provided the volunteers. The event featured fun games for kids of all ages and was designed to look like the Olympic Games. Volunteers from the church began building relationships as soon as parents arrived to register their children. Pastors from the church were also on hand helping with the games and meeting families. It was a very festive and high-energy celebration.

When the Olympic Torch approached, all the games were stopped and everyone was encouraged to line the street and cheer-on the Torch carriers. Once the Torch was out of sight the games resumed. The Torch provided a great focal point for promoting the event. All of the participants, their families and bank employees were invited to church activities specific to their age and interest. The church, the community, the bank and SOLA viewed this as a very positive event with great outreach value.

A great asset in planning a similar outreach (though not essential) is to have some official connection to the Torch Relay Route. The earlier you can obtain route information the easier your planning will be. Select churches that see the value in partnering with community entities and are good at being *light and salt* outside the walls of the church. Don't compromise your goal of building relationships with those outside the church as you partner with community organizations. You may not have the opportunity to verbally share the good news on the day of the Torch Relay, but if you prayerfully and intentionally invest in building relationships with people outside your church and strategically seek ways to stay in contact with these folks, you may be privileged to see God draw them to Jesus Christ. Light 'em up!

www.sportsoutreachla.org

9

AN AMERICAN
PERSPECTIVE

My life mission: to transform the latent energy of American
Christianity into active energy

Bob Buford

Dr Greg Linville is an accredited expert in the growth and
development of church sports and recreation ministry in the
United States and beyond. Awarded the world's first
Honorary Doctorate of Divinity in Sports Ministry from
Briercrest Seminary in Canada, he then gained a Doctorate
of Ministry with concentration in Sports Outreach from
Ashland Seminary in Ohio.

In his fifteen years as Director of Sports Outreach at First
Friends Evangelical Church in Ohio, his programmes
reached two thousand people each week through the
efforts of five hundred volunteers and a dozen staff and
interns. Presently he is the Executive Director of Church
Sports and Recreation Ministers (CSRM) and serves as
Assistant Professor of Sports Outreach Ministry at Malone
University. In this chapter, he shares the heart of his experience and research, discovering that the partnership
between sport and the Christian faith takes us 'beyond the
gold'.

1. The Case for Local Church Sports Outreach

Throughout history the church has utilized many ministry strategies in sharing the good news of Jesus. These include outreaches through art, music, dance, drama and social services. Sports outreach, however, has distinct advantages over other worthy endeavours.

a. Its relevance

Sport is relevant to reach the two missing groups of traditional churches: men and youth, who respond better to activity-based programmes. Anyone with teenagers will be familiar with the phrase 'bouncing off the walls', because adolescent energy levels are unparalleled and male hormones have been well documented as a biological cause for energizing men for activity.

Based on these assumptions, it should not be surprising to find most youth stop attending church shortly after church stops providing refreshments, recreation and activity-based learning. This disconnect usually occurs around the age of 10 or 11. Men, on the other hand, are attracted to churches that provide them with opportunities based on activity rather than verbal communication like preaching, teaching, singing or sharing. In activity-based contexts both men and young people find a particular attraction in following Christ.

Churches engaging in challenging and dynamic activities for youth and men will often grow solely because sports activities and sports facilities winsomely attract people. There is something special about seeing folk enjoying themselves with fun team games or families throwing balls and Frisbees around. Far more folk are initially at ease in this environment than they are in a church service, despite all its friendly notices or stunning architecture.

Sports activities provide continual marketing opportunities because of their modern day relevance. Local papers are desperate to take photographs of any event where people are enjoying themselves, especially if a church has organized the activity. News media look for innovative activities and fresh expressions of church. They are happy to find stories to alter perceptions of what being involved as a church member is all about.

b. It fulfils church growth principles

i. Sports ministry's main focus is outreach. Churches know outreach leads to growth but are often unaware of a very dangerous principle called 'maintenance creep'. The shift from outreach to pastoral care is often so subtle that most churches don't realize it is happening until it is too late. However, sports orientated activities keep churches at the cutting edge of society with activities naturally attractive to folk outside the church in ways unparalleled by any otherministry.

ii. Sports ministry provides a role for everyone. Traditionally the church is based upon verbal skills. Preaching, teaching, singing and sharing are all based on being verbal. Such activities are perfect for those gifted in communication. Not so much for those inclined to activity. Many non-verbal folk are excluded from serving or leading within a church because there are no responsibility posts for their skills. A sports outreach programme opens up new roles for many non-involved parishioners.

iii. Sport and recreation in the church provide a natural 'back-door' activity for church members to invite their family, friends and co-workers to. Most un-churched people aren't excited about invitations to come to church services. However, they do give serious thought to organized walks, keep-fit evenings and family fun days. The latter provides the ideal seedbed for relationships to blossom and deepen because sports events have regular fixture spots in the calendar. This is particularly significant when you consider it normally takes several years for a totally non-churched, secularized, non-believer to come to a personal faith in Christ. Most church outreaches last one hour, one day or, on rare occasions, one week. Sport keeps people involved for years and so greatly enhances a church's outreach success.

c. It has built-in accelerators

Statistics of how many people participate and are interested in sport and recreation fluctuate from country to country and year to year. But regardless of the year or place, the results are always the same – vast majorities of people participate in sports. Sport is the most relevant connection tool for churches wanting to reach a secular world.

Relationships naturally accelerate when the environment is sporting. It's a fact of life. Playing for a team for the first time may seem daunting but a common goal brings about an instant bonding few other areas of life can match. Without doubt, sport brings disparate people together quicker than any other ministry which means the accelerator of communicating faith is unparalleled. Sporting analogies, metaphors and experiences provide unique, insightful and relevant ways to communicate a personal and growing relationship with Christ. People are at their learning best whilst having fun. The Christian faith is better received by those engaged in activities they thoroughly enjoy.

d. It is cost effective

We live in an age where paying a goodly sum for a well-organized sporting activity is never frowned upon. Parents are only too delighted to find an activity week in the school holiday for their children to attend and think nothing of a weekly charge for swimming or judo lessons. By the same token, any church activity that is sport related can be assured its running will not be a pull on church budgets. In fact, it may well release funds for the employment of those with sporting expertise or for the purchase of suitable kit and prizes. When sponsorships from local businesses and tuck-shop revenues are added to activity fees, it is easy to see how sports ministries are far more cost effective and have a far greater potential for raising funds than any other ministry in the local church. Churches in both England and the United States have also received government grants to build facilities and administrate programmes.

2. Historical and Current Models of Local Church Sports Outreach

With the exponential growth of local church sports outreach ministry since 1990, it might be assumed church sports is a recent phenomena. Indeed, a dramatic increase has occurred in local church-based sports ministry over the last twenty years but examples of church sports ministry date back over the previous hundred years or so.

In America, the Southern Baptists have always played a leading role in church recreation as evidenced by over half of their 40,000 plus local congregations with athletic facilities.

Specific examples are varied. In a small Midwestern industrial city – Canton, Ohio – there has been local church sports ministry since at least 1912, when the city's very first gymnasium was built by the First United Church of Christ. From this early starting point, it is not surprising to find that

Canton continues to have a very large and energetic local church sports ministry community.

Beginning in the early twentieth century, First Christian Church of Canton, Ohio, built the first of five different campuses. Each new site increased the church's commitment to dedicated athletic facilities with the most recent being a golf course!

First Friends Church built its first gym in 1954 and serves thousands of community people each week in its various leagues and sports activities. Its large outdoor sports complex and its indoor gymnasium cum auditorium enables people to worship God six days a week through basketball, volleyball and other physical activities, at the same time as providing parishioners with a place to worship God in a more traditional way through multiple services each Sunday. The church grew from 400 to over 2,000 in the fifteen years after hiring a full-time Sports Outreach Pastor. These are just examples from nearly four dozen churches currently using sports ministries to reach the Canton community.

Memphis, Knoxville and Indianapolis each have at least four churches with athletic facilities worth at least one million dollars. Atlanta has seven such congregations. These churches staff these outreach facilities with a combination of full-time, part-time and volunteer workers. These facilities begin daily operation as early as 5:30 in the morning and remain open until 11:00 at night. All have basic facilities such as gymnasiums, track, game room, weight room, fitness centre, craft areas, snack or food service areas and office/administration space. Some go beyond this with such facilities as swimming pools, multiple gyms, bowling alleys and outdoor complexes.

Sports outreach, however, is not just for the 'mega-church'. Countless small churches throughout North America use a softball team, a youth league or an 'Uncharted Waters' summer sports camp as ways of engaging their own parishioners.

They also use these activities as a way of attracting non-churched friends, neighbours and family members. Their influence and impact can be observed by the example of Ron Keene, a long-time lay volunteer at North Benton Presbyterian Church. Located in a sparsely populated and rural community in north-eastern Ohio, the church averaged between 100–150 members and owned no athletic facilities. Yet, Ron organized church softball teams for years and later added a basketball team for the youth in his church. Without the advantages of 'mega' facilities, equipment or resources, Ron's efforts provided a solid foundation for North Benton Presbyterian to maintain its membership base and continue its outreach to the community. The results of his efforts will be fully known in heaven but there are enough earthly testimonies of 'changed lives', clearly indicating that even small unassuming local churches can have significant impact through a sports outreach programme.

Local Church Sports Outreach Outside of North America

Further chapters in this book will reveal the significance of the North Atlantic corridor in developing the partnership between the United States of America and the United Kingdom with respect to the growth of local church sports ministry. Both have much to offer each other and both are on the cusp of exciting and accelerating growth in this millennium. The chapter on 'Sports Ministries at Home and Abroad' will give you some flavour of this progress.

3. Sporting Trends

Trends come and go. Local churches should always be aware of trends and try to capitalize on them, but also recognize that a programme built upon a trend will have a 'shelf life' and should avoid committing large amounts of resources to endeavours or facilities that cannot be adapted to future trends. What follows are my observations of trends within local church sports outreach. They are based upon decades of consulting with hundreds of local churches.

a. Generational trends

One of the most significant trends amongst the boomer and millennial generations has been a movement towards recreation and personal fitness while participation in team sports has declined.

In addition, 'echo boomers' (under 20 years of age) tend to prefer individualized electronic leisure pursuits and seem to be rejecting competition more than previous generations. Despite this, participation in youth sports leagues continues to rise – particularly for pre-teenage school ages. I predict, however, that youth-based team sports will plateau for the following reasons:

i. The elimination of competition
One of the main reasons teenage team sports are declining is the fallout from a movement to eliminate competition from youth sports. League officials no longer keep scores or standings and, in addition, every participant is 'awarded' with the same trophy, regardless of their effort, skill or accomplishment. If everyone is a winner, sport loses its purpose and enjoyment.

ii. The general trend towards self actualization

Personal experience is more important than a team accomplishment. More and more youth are attracted to sporting activity maximizing individual involvement such as the 'three Bs' – Boards, Bikes and Blades.

Team sports experiencing huge increases in participation such as Ultimate Frisbee are popular because they are not strictly supervised or administrated. Younger millennials (20–35-year-olds) and older echo boomers (15–19-year-olds) enjoy the sport of 'Ultimate' because it accentuates individual efforts, rewards 'style points' as much as or more than a 'win' and perhaps, most importantly, the competition is not under the strict supervision and direction of adults.

Individualized recreation being on the increase is also evidenced by huge increases in 'sidewalk' leisure pursuits: biking, rollerblading, cross-country skiing, jogging and hiking. In addition, the fastest growing parkland being purchased and developed is linear – ten feet wide and miles long. Personal training is also at an all time high.

b. Other relevant social trends

i. Rising electronic 'connectivity' and rising illiteracy

Within five years, the vast majority of children 18 and under will have been electronically 'connected' their entire life having always owned a personal electronic communication device. These devices make proper spelling and reading irrelevant since 'it takes too long to spell everything out' on small hand-held iPhones. Computer-based spell and grammar checks also facilitate illiteracy. Is it any wonder America will soon have more school children who are unable to read and write than those who can? Local church youth leagues leaders should be concerned because a large part of their ministry depends upon participants reading Scripture, devotionals and/or famous athletes' testimonies.

ii. Sunday concerns
More youth play in Sunday morning soccer leagues than attend Sunday school and so erode a vital and strong spiritual foundation.

iii. Outdoor pursuits continue to thrive
Record numbers of recreational vehicles, boats and outdoor recreational equipment are being purchased, even in this down economy time. This serves to take more and more families away from church during holidays and vacations.

iv. Sport has reached a plateau
Both the Vancouver Winter Olympics and the South African Soccer World Cup ventures struggled financially, whilst the broadcast network for the Olympics estimated a loss of twenty million dollars. A lack of true 'sporting role models' together with obscene amounts of money paid to 'pampered' athletes are both contributory factors to a growing disillusionment with sport.

c. Overall church trends

i. Growth of the mega church
Between three and four hundred American churches close their doors each month. In addition, over 50 per cent of the people who attend a worship service each week do so at less than 12 per cent of the church sites. This explains the 'mega church' phenomenon that has proliferated North America during the last twenty years. Yet even the 'mega church' movement may have peaked as there is now a distinct move among the 'twenty-somethings' towards a less

institutionalized, more 'house church' style community of faith.

A key to the growth of many mega churches consists of their ability to replace the 'neighbourhood' of the 1950s–1970s with their pseudo-neighbourhood, which not only provides a safe environment for children and families but also enables social networking of 'like-values' people. Additional services include athletics, coffee-shops, counselling and lending libraries. Many even offer a school and/or work co-operatively with the growing home-school industry in the area of physical education.

ii. Growth of multi-site churches

A united church organization often oversees multiple ministry sites, each with its own building, leadership team and services. The uniting factor is typically the lead pastor who preaches via electronic links at various sites. Some churches have satellite sites in multiple states and countries.

iii. Gender and church leadership

The broader church has seen a major leadership shift from men to women. Many main line denominations have 50 per cent or more of their local parishes led by women, particularly in rural and urban settings. Seminary attendance continues to see the percentage of women increase with women regularly outnumbering men in some. A key fact about churches which target men is that they regularly report significant growth – often explosive growth.

iv. Worship wars

'Contemporary worship' is at least thirty years old and should now be officially termed 'traditional', while what has been called traditional should be considered classical. Churches embracing a style 'beyond contemporary', will attract echo-boomers. Congregations tapping into the individualism of the new generation and offering community-based approaches to outreach and discipleship will continue to grow.

4. Church Trends Provide Opportunities

Mega churches should be embraced because they have the 'critical mass' necessary to build state-of-the-art athletic facilities which winsomely attract the non-churched. With the loss of safe neighbourhoods and secular youth athletics erring on one of two ends of a continuum (either de-emphasizing competition or tolerating overzealous coaches, parents and leagues which more resemble child-abuse than coaching) local churches have an opportunity to be a true beacon for the entire community. Great potential abounds for culture-shapers. When many churches are struggling to be attractive to men, those with energetic sports and recreational departments will attract men and keep them involved.

a. Trends within local church sports outreach

i. Missional outreach
To be missional is imperative. Instead of administrating 'in house' youth or adult leagues, some churches challenge church members to participate and coach in community leagues so as to be 'salt and light'.

ii. Relational evangelism
Churches are experiencing more fruit from investing in long-term relational outreaches than from 'big event' styled evangelism based upon 'big name' athletes or coaches speaking at one-off events.

iii. Enhancing the verbal proclamation

When experienced speakers give huddle talks before, during or after games and recreational activities, the verbal proclamation of the gospel is significantly enhanced.

iv. Social networking

Social networking to communicate, recruit and/or proclaim the gospel message pays higher dividends each year.

b. Concerns about these trends within sports outreach

i. Problems with the missional approach

The missional approach of challenging laity to go and be 'salt and light' is wonderful in concept but often dismal in reality because . . .

- Laity are inspired to go out but are not equipped, trained nor held accountable.
- Laity are often a 'lone voice' in a very secular setting and, while personally remaining faithful, they are often not fruitful due to the hostile environment.
- A certain 'critical mass' is necessary for true fruit to be borne.
- Churches sending out laity rarely build natural conduits or bridges from the secular leagues back to the local church.

ii. Problems with the 'big event'

Evangelism based upon enabling parishioners to build long-term relationships with non-churched people is far more effective than outreach based on one-time events. However, even though the 'big name/big event' style of evangelism has inherent limitations when it is the only strategy used, it is unwise to never utilize it. A well-planned event within an overall, long-term evangelism strategy based upon a relational approach can be quite effective.

iii. Problems with using 'experienced' speakers
There are real advantages to having gifted, experienced and trained voices share the gospel message within sports outreaches, but the great asset of bumbling, yet sincere, testimonies from respected teammates or coaches should not be unappreciated.

c. One church's experience at becoming a trendsetter

Twenty-five years ago, one particular church determined it wanted to become a *culture shaper and trendsetter* in youth sport basketball. Two years of research on the physiological, psychological, emotional, sociological and spiritual development of youth sport participants revealed:

- Children mature at different rates physiologically, and thus boys who are 8 years old chronologically, could be anywhere between 5 and 11 years old physiologically.
- Sociologically, children desire fun and friendships over pressured competition.
- Emotionally, children can be scarred by traumatic competitive experiences.
- Psychologically, younger aged children are not capable of processing the myriad of complex stimuli and pressures brought about by intense competition.
- Spiritually, children are very open to being moulded in their character and values through competition.

With this information, the church set out to redesign their youth leagues, which included organizing youth sport participants into leagues based upon the physiological, psychological and emotional maturation of players rather than by grade or age. In addition, adjustments to the facility included investing in adjustable height basketball goals, shortening courts and using smaller balls – all designed to be more conducive to the physiological maturation of the participants. A systematic   curriculum of progressive skills was created and taught to coaches via coaches' clinics. Coaches in turn taught and drilled players in these fundamentals. Coaches were also trained in the psychological, emotional, sociological and spiritual stages of development for the age group they coached. This training included techniques, specific mannerisms, words and attitudes appropriate for the youth they were developing.

The response of those involved in the leagues was initially very negative. Parents believed lower goals and smaller courts would retard athletic development, and many of them pulled their children out of the leagues. However, it became apparent that boys were not only developing basketball skills, but were also developing the character needed to be successful in sports and also in life. This 'experiment' changed the entire youth basketball culture. Twenty-five years later, every youth league in the surrounding area had adopted the basic philosophy of the church!

Will you and your church embrace the challenge to be culture shapers and trendsetters? What sport or recreational activity in your community needs to be 'transformed'?

5. Vision to Reality

a. Seven tasks

Seven tasks are needed to make Sports Outreach in a local church a reality.

i. Establish the vision, mission, strategies and activities

Unless evangelism is intentional, it is accidental at best. Vision is not the same as mission. Both are different than a statement of purpose, a guiding principle or strategy. Vision is what is 'seen' when the mission has been accomplished. Vision is a descriptive noun whereas mission is a verb. Mission describes the activity needed to accomplish the vision. A vision can emerge from a statement of purpose or a guiding principle but is distinctively different. For example, the Honda Company's vision of 'twelve Hondas in every garage' clearly describes a 'visual' end result. Honda's mission then becomes to create twelve affordable motorized machines (think cars and motorcycles, but also lawnmowers, weed-whackers, etc.).

A vision statement should be short and clear, usually one sentence or phrase. A mission statement could be a sentence or two but it is at its best when succinct. Unless the vision can be quickly said and easily remembered it will not be an effective guide.

Strategies further define the mission and give it physical expression. Strategies have more to do with the programmatic philosophies of the organization as distinguished from the activities (outputs) of the organization.

To summarize, a vision is 'the shore being sailed to'; the mission is the 'task of sailing' and possible strategies could be to use 'oars, sails or motors'.

For local churches, the shore (vision) could be 'redeemed lives and a redeemed culture'. The sailing (mission) could be 'to create a relevant, attractive and interactive outreach to the unchurched community'. The 'oar' (strategy) could be youth sport outreaches, and the specific activities (outputs) would be leagues, camps and clinics. Hopefully, these outputs result in seeing the vision of 'redeemed lives' becoming a reality ('outcome').

Key: Unless a vision statement can be easily remembered and quickly said, it will not be an effective guide.

ii. Research – 'Failing to prepare means you are preparing to fail'

- Vision, mission, strategies and activities are best determined when based upon research. To do proper research, local churches must first define a target community. Who are they called to reach out to? A combination of their geographic and demographic communities will provide the basis for the research. For example: 'This church is called to serve all who reside between this river and that mountain and will target in particular, 25–45-year-old men and their families.' After the community has been defined the research begins . . .
- The next step is to compare community needs with church resources. For example, the targeted community may have a large youth football programme but nothing for youth basketball. It may have a large adult tennis programme but nothing for adult rugby. Church resources might include the following: a) the facility of a sports hall/gymnasium but no outdoor fields/pitches; b) parishioners who have playing and coaching experience in basketball and rugby, but none in tennis and only a few in football. The 'map' which has just been drawn would indicate that the strategy to reach the pre-determined community would involve developing youth basketball and adult rugby outreaches.

iii. Establish strategies – 'Be relevant or be marginalized'
Research indicated relevant strategies of youth basketball and adult rugby. Further considerations include:

- What time of year (spring, summer, winter).
- What format (league, camp, clinic).
- What philosophy (highly competitive, instructional, recreational, etc.).

iv. Recruit and train leadership – 'Produce reproducing leaders'
A series of four questions help determine whether or not churches should enter into a particular strategy/activity:

- Will this specific strategy accomplish our vision?
- Do we have leadership for this activity?
- Do we have finances for this activity?
- Can this activity be accommodated in our facilities and schedule?

Obviously, a church should not continue on any venture that doesn't fulfil its vision, but it is just as important to stop any forward movement if there is no leadership! The key to any successful ministry outreach is its ability to enable church members to develop long-term relationships with those outside of the church. This assumes the leadership of any outreach will come from church members.

Recruiting leaders takes many forms and must be actively engaged in by the pastoral staff. Corporate tasks include spoken and written invitations during weekly services, notices in church newsletters, emails and all electronic social networks. In addition, sermons, personal testimonies and/or dramatic presentations during weekly services are especially effective. However, nothing takes the place of prayer and personal recruitment . . .

Recruitment begins with a 'workers list'. Church leaders create a list of potential leaders and 'ask the Lord of the harvest, therefore, to send out workers' (Matthew 9:38). The prayer is followed up with a letter of invitation which includes all particular details, dates, responsibilities, roles and commitments, and, most of all, the vision. Recruitment letters are followed with a personal call or visit.

> Model it – Watch me do it
> Monitor it – We'll do it together
> Mentor it – I'll watch you do it
> Manage it – I'm here if you need me

One key to ensure continued leaders is to establish a 'leader in training' approach. Every leader (coach) is assigned one or two assistants, who understand that they are 'in training' to be a head coach in the coming years. This is greatly enhanced if head coaches take responsibility to recruit their own assistants. This three- to four-year concept is succinctly described in the side bar.

Training and preparation for all current leaders are often the most overlooked aspects of recruiting new leaders! Leaders who are adequately prepared (and because of that preparation will experience success), will provide the most enthusiastic 'word of mouth' recruiting a church can get.

A curriculum for training should consist of a three-year rotation of the following:

- Coaching in a Christmanship ethic.
- Relational and lifestyle evangelism.
- Personal discipleship for full spiritual maturity.

Additional yearly organizational meetings to outline expectations are essential.

Trained coaches that experience personal growth and success in reaching players for Christ naturally reproduce themselves.

v. Risk management – 'Friends don't sue friends'
The two ministries most exposed to lawsuits are youth and sports ministry. One traffic accident involving a youth group bus can result in millions of dollars/pounds worth of liability. People participating in sport can suffer catastrophic injuries and death. Adhering to the following check list can greatly aid in providing a safe and friendly environment.

- Provide an 'informed consent' form.
- Require doctor's physicals for participants.
- Train all coaches and volunteers in first aid and CPR.
- Require certifications for all health and aerobics instructors.
- Require certifications for all youth coaches.
- Require background checks for all youth coaches.
- Maintain an up-to-date first aid kit and any other medical device such as a defibrillator.
- Have a yearly facilities inspection by local emergency medical squad.
- Be on a 'first name' basis with each of your participants.

The most important part of keeping a sports ministry out of legal difficulties is to treat and interact with each of your participants as Christ would. His love for them would be evidenced in the inspection of each playing surface and facility; screening, training and monitoring of each coach; attainment of the highest quality first aid care and equipment available.

Each country, state, county and municipality has different legalities when it comes to liability. It is recommended that you work this through with a local attorney and/or solicitor.

vi. Administration – 'Organization that maximizes connections'
Churches need to view and administrate sports outreach the same way all other ministries of the church are administered. The director of the ministry should meet all ministry standards including:

- Ordination, licensing or recording.
- A theological and/or ministerial degree.
- Being held to the same standards and expectation as all other staff. They should also receive the same pay and benefits.

Beyond the commonalities of ministry, the uniqueness of sports outreach needs to be comprehended. Sports staff will work different hours, different days and have different busy seasons. Accommodations as to meeting times and staff interactions will be necessary.

Most importantly, a concerted effort to integrate the sports ministry into a whole church outreach strategy will pay huge dividends. There is often a 'disconnect' between the sports programmes of a church and the rest of the church's ministries.

vii. Evaluation – 'What doesn't get checked doesn't get done'
Yearly and seasonal evaluations will enhance the accomplishment of the vision. Each activity, each staff person and each volunteer must be evaluated to see if everything has been successful and what improvements can be made.

Staff should be evaluated by supervisors, by those they supervise and even by volunteers every three months for the first year and yearly afterwards.

Volunteers should be evaluated after each cycle of ministry. This evaluation should come from the supervising staff and also include evaluations filed by participants and/or parents of participants of teams they coach, leagues they supervise or activities they oversee.

Staff and key volunteers should meet after each cycle of ministry to assemble all the various evaluations and use them as the basis for planning the next season or year. An important part of this evaluation is the assessment of whether or not the current strategies and activities are truly relevant and effective in accomplishing the vision of the sports outreach.

6. Summary

Churches can be confident that a well-thought-out and organized sports outreach programme can indeed be a catalyst for attaining their goal of reaching and discipling those in their community that are not yet Christians. The philosophy of using sport as an evangelistic tool is solidly based upon a theological foundation and rests upon successful historical precedents. Churches will grow and flourish if they adhere to the principles and examples outlined within this chapter.

10

PASSING ON
THE TORCH

I must cultivate a spiritual life that covers the entire distance

Gordon McDonald

In his book *Many Aspire, Few Attain*, Walter A. Henrichsen tells of his time at jungle camp when he used to go on survival hikes. He would build a campfire and sleep around it in his lean-to since it was the flame that kept the animals at bay. Even then he could still see their eyes but, thankfully, they were at a considerable distance. As the fire grew dim during the night, these animals got braver and came closer so it was imperative that Walter kept alert and regularly built-up and stoked the fire.

So it is in our lands that the eyes of the evil one come ever closer as the fires of evangelical Christianity appear to be losing their heat. With the sin of greed, affluence, permissiveness and other selfish pursuits advancing, it is the Christian's calling to keep the torch burning for Jesus. As the Olympic torch is passed from hand to hand and nation to nation every four years, so sports ministry must seek to leave an enduring legacy that will not only change lives but take them on to Christian maturity and discipleship.

Sports Discipleship

In many ways, sport provides the ideal environment for leading people to Christ and then training them as disciples. Those you meet will generally enjoy company, be outgoing and open to life sharing. The problem with sports ministry in many churches is that it does a good job with sports but rarely makes the transition to ministry. Organizing activities solely to make relationships is good up to a point, but every programme needs to include times where the Christian message is spelt out and the way is made clear for the participants to receive Christ for themselves. Otherwise, there is no difference between the church activity and the sports club down the road. The plus factor of the Cross must underpin all your plans and aspirations.

I remember many years ago benefiting as a student from the ministry of the Navigators and their remarkable attention to detail in discipleship training. The new Christian was always encouraged to spend a good year with the person who had led him to Christ so they could pray and read the Bible together and help each other on to Christian maturity in the lifestyle they shared. Jesus himself gave so much attention to discipleship that he spent three very full years building into the lives of men and women who were to advance the Kingdom of God to its next stage. He knew the value of having a small squad of believers, taught to be prayer warriors, soaked in scriptural truth and obedient to the leading of the Holy Spirit. It wasn't surprising that they gained a reputation for turning the world upside down.

The success of the Alpha Course over the last decade in introducing vast numbers of people to the claims of Christ and the life-changing power of the Holy Spirit has been largely due to the convivial atmosphere created in a non-threatening environment. Alpha has allowed its participants to absorb ideas, voice their thoughts and observe Christ in the lives of others. In similar fashion, a sport and recreation programme should have inbuilt into it an 'investigating Christian belief' course that is user-friendly to sports people. This means that any presentation of the gospel can be followed by an invitation to enquirers to join the course. The following 'Race of Life' study is an example of a four-week course that would take such enquirers through the basic foundations of the Christian life and provide them with the opportunity to come to faith themselves. Each week requires a little background reading on the part of the participant so that a mixture of sharing and teaching can take place. The material is such that it can be covered adequately in one hour. Organizing a buffet-style meal around the topic under discussion can only assist in the forging of relationships and the flow of conversation. Copies of the study booklet can be obtained from Higher Sports.

In seeking to convince his readers of the refreshing challenge found in the Christian life, the Apostle Paul made frequent references to 'running the race'. He encouraged the Christians at Philippi to keep their focus on 'what is ahead' as they 'pressed towards the goal' and sought to 'win the prize'. He believed there was a 'race marked out', a race both demanding and exciting, with a throbbing stadium beckoning the runners who completed the distance.

The investigator can study the role Jesus plays as confidant and coach

These studies consider what is required of the spiritual athlete in the Race of Life. The resurrection of Jesus is examined as the gateway into the Race, together with other pre-race requisites. The investigator can study the role

Jesus plays as confidant and coach and begin to understand something of the training schedule mapped out for the Christian athlete.

A final comparison with athletes who have 'completed the course' gives a true sense of both the challenge in starting the Race and the eternal significance in finishing it.

Study 1 - The Race Conditions

'I press on towards the goal to win the prize'

Philippians 3:14

No serious athlete enters a race unless he knows what is required of him. A full investigation of the race conditions is called for. This is also the case with entry into the Kingdom of God.

The *events* surrounding the life of Jesus are both amazing and unique. God himself in the person of Jesus Christ stepped into human history. Much is at stake on the strength of this assertion and so it is vital for us to take a long and unbiased look at the surrounding facts.

Resurrection

Read some of the gospel accounts of the resurrection: John chapter 20, Luke chapter 24.

How did different people react to the resurrection of Jesus?
See Matthew 28:1-15, Acts 5:25-32, Acts 17:16-23,32.

Are there other possible explanations for the empty tomb?

Bottom line

Why do you think Christian belief hinges on the truth of the resurrection of Jesus?

What is your personal opinion at this stage?

Reliable or what?

The New Testament was written between AD 48 and AD 110. Records go back to as early as AD 120 and are found in over 4,000 Greek texts and many more in other ancient languages. By comparison, the details of Caesar's Gallic Wars (58 BC–50 BC) are only found in a handful of manuscripts, the earliest of which was written around AD 900. No keen scholar of history would doubt the authenticity of the latter!

A further question . . .

Can I be sure that the New Testament writers were telling the truth and had not been deceived by the lies of others?

Investigate their statements and claims:

Luke 1:1–4
Comment_____

2 Peter 1:16
Comment_____

The Apostle Paul had a life-changing experience when he had a personal encounter with Jesus Christ. It led him to assert, '[Jesus Christ] declared with power to be the Son of God, by his resurrection from the dead' (Romans 1:4).

Conclusion

If Jesus rose from the dead and he is still alive today, then it must be possible for us to know him. The next study examines closely how this relationship can be forged.

Study 2 – Beginning the Race

> 'Let us fix our eyes on Jesus, the author and perfecter of our faith'
>
> Hebrews 12:2

The point of entry into the Christian life starts with the Race of Life. Jesus is exceptionally qualified to be the Starter of the Race.

Discuss the following statements:

- He has experienced the Race for himself (Hebrews 12:2).
- He knows intimately all the pitfalls (Hebrews 4:15).
- Only he knows the way to the stadium (John 14:6).
- He will be at the finishing tape (Philippians 3:14).

Once we begin to accept the claims Jesus made about himself, we then hit stormy weather concerning his death.

Why did he have to die?

1. It was part of God's plan.
   Examine 1 Peter 1:10–12 and Hebrews 1:1–2.

'But you, Bethlehem Ephrathah, though you are small among the clans of Judah, out of you will come for me one who will be ruler over Israel, whose origins are from old, from ancient times' (Micah 5:2, prophet, c.700 BC).

2.Jesus predicted it.
  See Mark 9:30–32.

  What did Jesus chose to do?
  John 10:17–18 --

3.It was God's way of rescuing mankind.
  Read 1 Peter 3:18.
  What did Jesus die for? ----------------------------
  Who did Jesus die for? -----------------------------
  What was the result of his death? ------------------

Our Race entry form has been signed by Jesus. Without his sacrifice we are ineligible to compete (1 John 5:12).

Is it time to start the Race?

The Bible gives 4 steps you must consider:

- Admit you are a sinner and have a need of God (Rom. 3:23).
- Believe (trust) in Jesus Christ (Romans 10:9).
- Consider the relative costs and the rewards (John 3:16 and Luke 8:34,35).
- Do it! . . . Decide to put Jesus first in your life (John 1:12).

You could say a prayer like this:

> Lord Jesus Christ
> I know I have sinned in my thoughts, words and actions.
> There are so many good things I have not done.
> Please forgive me and help me to turn from every-
> thing I know to be wrong.
> You gave your life on the Cross for me and now I
> gladly give my life to you.
> Come in to be my Saviour, Lord and Friend and fill me
> now with you Spirit.
> Amen

You have now started the Race of Life. Never doubt the day Jesus started you off. There will be tough days ahead but Jesus promises to be your constant running companion (Hebrews 13:5,8).

Enjoy the Run . . . there is a great finish!

Study 3 – The Training Programme

'Everyone who competes in the games goes into strict training'

1 Corinthians 9:25

Jesus Christ can enter your life and forgive you immediately but it will take a lifetime for your character to be transformed 'into his likeness' (2 Corinthians 3:18).

The dedicated athlete knows that an all-year-round training programme is essential for peak fitness. The

Christian athlete must seek to keep his spiritual life in the fitness zone where it will grow strong and healthy.

Consider 5 areas where the 'disciple' (a learner in training) can make good progress in his spiritual fitness:

1. Keep up the intake level (Bible study)

Discuss how 2 Timothy 3:16 can be fully implemented.

2. Be a good team player (Fellowship)

a.   What did Jesus have to say about our relationships with others? (John 13:34,35)
b.   Might there be some adjustments in priorities? (Philippians 2:3,4)
c.   Why is it so important to meet with other believers? (Hebrews 10:24,25)

3. Play up front (Telling others)

Simon of Cyrene identified with Jesus in the public place (Luke 23:26). How can Christians take up the Cross and follow Jesus? (Romans 1:16)
Why might you be ashamed of being a Christian?

4. Communicate regularly with the Coach (Prayer)

Look at Philippians 4:6,7.
What does this mean on a daily basis?

5. Do the business on match day (Achieving goals)

Consider what bearing fruit involves (John 15:8).
Very few athletes manage to remain at the top by relying on natural ability only. A disciplined approach to training is vital. Getting the pulse rate into the target zone at regular intervals has many benefits.

- It increases the blood supply to the muscles.
- It increases the number of blood capillaries around the heart, thereby strengthening it.
- Increases the aerobic capacity of the body.

In the same way, the spiritual athlete needs to 'breathe in' the presence of God (Bible study, prayer, fellowship, faith sharing) at regular intervals in order to keep his 'heart' (inner being) in God's target zone.

What benefits do you think can come from this?

Study 4 - Maintaining the Pace

'Run with perseverance the race marked out'

Hebrews 12:1

Many talented athletes have not made the grade because their skill level was not matched by determination and endurance. Many aspire, few attain! The Tokyo-produced documentary of Abibe Bikila's Marathon victory in the 1964 Olympics was a case in point. The camera closely followed the Ethiopian for every step of his journey and clearly illustrated the discipline required to cope with all aspects of the race. Other athletes were seen sitting down at the drinks station and obtaining lifts back to the stadium whilst Bikila's eyes were firmly fixed on the stadium.

What does the Bible have to say about maintaining pace in the Christian's life?

Philippians 3:12–14 _____

Hebrews 12:1–3 _____

Hebrews 12:7,12 _____

Discuss what obstacles you are likely to encounter as you press on in the Christian faith (Hebrews 3:12).

Eric Liddell in the film *Chariots of Fire* is remembered for his dedication to the spiritual race as well as the physical one (gold medal in the 1924 Olympics for the 400 metres, and rugby union caps for Scotland as a winger). What many do not know is that he ended his life in a Japanese internment camp where his love and care for others belied his own physical hardships. As a dedicated spiritual athlete, he continued to rise before dawn and meet with his eternal coach. He had the stadium in his sights and he was not going to falter.

Consider the Race that Abraham ran in Hebrews 11:8–10.
How did it start?
Where was the course?
What was his race attitude?
Where was he heading for?

What encourages the spiritual athlete daily in his relationship with Jesus Christ, his personal coach? (Revelation 21:5–7)

Review

Record three things about the Race of Life that you believe God has spoken to you about during these studies:
1----------------------
2----------------------
3----------------------
Remember, Jesus runs with you . . . always (Matthew 28:20).

There is little doubt that a sport and recreation programme will make inroads into any local community in ways no other church programme can achieve. Many American churches would attribute their quantum growth leaps to the success of their sports ministry. My visit to Willow Creek Church near Chicago in Illinois in the late 90s revealed a sports department that had 122 basketball teams operating in their inter-mural league. The programme was for the men of the church and their friends, and sought to transport the players from the gymnasium to the sanctuary through friendship evangelism. It may seem an obvious point to make but sports ministry must be geared to men and women, boys and girls being reborn into God's Kingdom. It is then that the fun starts.

A sport and recreation programme will make inroads into any local community in ways no other church programme can achieve ⌒

Taking a new Christian through to mature discipleship is not a strategy that the local church always has high on its list. Fortunately, it was high on Jesus' list and became a vital part of his final instructions to his disciples since they were clearly told to 'go and make disciples' throughout the world. They had Jesus as a role model and from the word 'go' gave close attention to nurturing individual growth.

The methodology of discipleship is all important and in this respect certain statistics can be quite staggering. Should an evangelist reach one person a day, then 11,680 people would be reached in thirty-two years. If each new discipler trains one person a year to become a discipler himself, then the number grows to 4,294,967,296 in the same period of time.

The sports ministry environment provides the ideal setting for discipleship training. To play a part in leading someone to Christ is exciting enough, but then to spend the next year helping that person grow in his faith is unbelievably rewarding. Praying and studying the Bible together, sharing faith together, playing sport together and enjoying a meal together are all times when the disciple learns the rudiments of becoming a mature believer in Christ and playing a part in bringing others to that same point. Indeed, the two goals of discipleship would be for the disciple to become a 'self-feeder' and then a 'reproducer'.

The sports ministry environment provides the ideal setting for discipleship training

Discipleship Strategy

Like any effective sports ministry programme, discipleship planning and strategy does not happen naturally. It requires prayer and practical design. The potential to teach, train and transmit within an environment that is Christ centred cannot be over emphasized. The teaching moments can make reality out of theory with spiritual analogies from every day sporting activities. Training consists of instruction that can then be repeated and reinforced through regular contact together. Finally, there is the challenging responsibility of demonstrating the Christian life. In many ways, the discipler's attitude on the field of play and in pressure situations can have a greater influence than the day's Bible study together. To see the 'walk' match the 'talk' can often be the breakthrough time for the disciple.

The world of sport and recreation is a great instructional area for the fresh disciple. There is so much in the rules and the manner of sport that can be looked at parabolically, as earthly situations are seen in the light of heavenly meanings. Paul the Apostle moved in a Greek society that focused a lot of its attention on physical fitness and games competitions. Like Jesus before him, Paul took the interests of the day and used them as a platform for instruction. Sport itself provides for the Christian participant a spiritual laboratory where the trying and testing of faith is an ongoing process. Spiritual progress or otherwise can often be measured by reaction and temperament on the sports field, and the discipleship situation is the ideal place to address both. To be able to put failure to live up to God's standards against the back cloth of 2 Timothy 3:16 ('teaching, rebuking, correcting and training in righteousness') is an important part of the process of growth. However, perhaps the greatest area of instruction for the new disciple is that of personal accountability. The writer of Proverbs gives helpful advice when he notes that 'wounds from a friend can be trusted' (Proverbs 27:6) and 'as iron sharpens iron, so one man sharpens another' (Proverbs 27:17). To be prepared to let another watch your back and comment on the most personal and sensitive of issues is also to let the Holy Spirit instruct your innermost character.

Once you are living the gospel, then it becomes such a short step to inspire others with its message

The final part of the discipleship strategy is that of modelling and mentoring. As Jesus moved around Galilee, he was incarnational not informational. He didn't just bring news from heaven; he brought heaven itself down to the lives of men and women. If you wanted to know about God, you looked at Jesus and saw how he dealt with people and safeguarded his time with his heavenly Father. The discipler has got to live the Christian life knowing that his friends will take their cue from what they see of God in him. Once you are living the gospel, then it becomes such a short step to inspire others with its message.

I owe a lot to the Navigator organization for its discipleship programme in my own life as a young schoolteacher. The building blocks of Bible study, prayer, fellowship and witnessing were constantly impressed, repeated and reinforced in my life and are the foundations that I am still able to stand on. What an impact would be felt in the community if sports ministry disciples from the local church systematically sought to disciple others in the ways of God. Then God's kingdom would be seen to be growing at pace. The torch wouldn't be in any danger of growing dim and the church of Christ would be operating effectively *beyond the gold*.

11

MORE THAN GOLD

Your faith will be like gold that has been tested in a fire. And these trials will prove that your faith is worth much more than gold
1 Peter 1:7 (CEV)

At the time of writing, the London Olympic Games are approaching fast, and soon churches and schools will be looking for ways that they can contribute to this once-in-a-lifetime opportunity. The organization More Than Gold exists primarily to engage people with the Games in a strategic and coordinated way.

How it All Began

The Christian community has been involved with the world's sporting events for over forty years. In the early years, denominations and agencies worked independently of each other but then, in the 1980s and early 1990s, a number of sports mission agencies helped the local churches develop partnerships. This then made it possible for the churches to offer a wide range of officially sanctioned initiatives including:

- Giving out water to the crowds.
- Hosting athletes' families.

- Providing thousands of volunteers.
- Providing chaplains in the athletes' villages.
- Staging events with creative arts performers.
- Contributing literature resources.

Then Came More Than Gold

In the build up to the 1996 Atlanta Games, an umbrella Christian agency, Quest Atlanta, saw the need for a uniting name and identity which would provide:

- A flag for faith-based outreach, hospitality and service without overstepping any denominational or doctrinal boundaries.
- An interface between the sports event's organizing committee and the churches.

As a result, More Than Gold has been used by the Christian community since the 1996 Atlanta Summer Games at numerous multi sport major events around the world including:

- Commonwealth Games
- Pan American Games
- All-Africa Games
- South Pacific Games
- Indian Ocean Games
- Olympic Games and Paralympics.

This has led to churches playing an ever-increasing role in assisting the official local organizing committee to implement programmes associated with the Games.

The Origin of More Than Gold UK

A series of key events led to the establishment of More Than Gold in the UK:

- In July 2005, the world learned that London was to be the host city for the 2012 Olympics and Paralympics. Immediately, Christian leaders began to discuss their response to this unprecedented opportunity.
- In March 2006, a number of denominations and organizations met to discuss the establishment of More Than Gold as a key way to engage with the Games.
- In January 2007, More Than Gold was launched at Westminster Central Hall. Those present included Tessa Jowell, MP and Minister for Sport and the Games, Archbishop Rowan Williams and Archbishop Cormack Murphy-O'Connor.
- In 2008, More Than Gold was established as a Charitable Trust under the chairmanship of Lord Brian Mawhinney, with the CEO, David Willson, appointed later that year.
- In July 2009, the vision was launched to over 300 leaders from denominations and organizations which met at Wembley Stadium for the More Than Gold Engagement Conference. At this conference More Than Gold shared its initial goals for the Games:

  1. Establish venue prayer walks, 24/7 boiler rooms and festivals of prayer involving 30,000 plus people.
  2. Provide housing and logistic support for 30 official chaplains.
  3. Provide 500 homes to host athlete family members.
  4. Recruit 5,000 people to serve as volunteers.
  5. Recruit 200 churches to assist with the staging of the Torch Relay across the UK.

6. Distribute 1,000,000 cups of refreshment to spectators during the Games.
7. Stage 2,000 creative arts performances across the UK.
8. Provide Bible-based sports programming for 10,000 youth across the UK.
9. Establish ongoing sports missions at 100 churches.
10. Co-ordinate the production and distribution of 1,000,000 sports-related resources.
11. Recruit 3,000 plus churches across the UK to partner with More Than Gold programmes.
12. Provide hospitality to 10,000 plus visitors and locals via centres.
13. Recruit 300 plus churches to participate in programmes dealing with homelessness, human trafficking and creation care.
14. Recruit 200 churches to stage 100 big screen festivals across the country.
15. Recruit, train, host and provide programming opportunities for 5,000 service team members in partnership with local churches.
16. Establish a systematic follow-up and discipleship programme for the tens of thousands of people touched by More Than Gold programmes.

Church Engagement with the Games

Whether the local church is in the heart of London or hundreds of miles away, there are many different ways of engaging with the Games. To reflect this, More Than Gold has established a number of teams to help co-ordinate the planning and delivery of programmes across all denominations and Christian organizations. There are many sports ministries, described in another part of this book, that have played key roles in working with More Than Gold to this end.

Partnership

More Than Gold's role is to help churches, organizations and individuals inspired by their faith to step up to the mark and serve in radical ways during the Games. In partnership with over 100 agencies and denominations and thousands of Christians, More Than Gold will serve as a catalyst to:

- *Cast vision* and encourage UK Christians with the stories and lessons from previous Games.
- *Connect Christians* across the country and across the globe for the purpose of developing unity, plans and programmes.
- *Co-ordinate* the production and delivery of programmes and resources on a national and local community level.

Outreach teams – reaching beyond the church walls

For many churches, figuring out how to engage in sports ministry is a bit of a mystery. The Outreach Programme Teams will provide training, resources and services to help churches reach beyond their walls.

The *Sports Mission Team* will help to support current Christian athletes and encourage churches to reach out to sportspeople interested in the Christian faith. Their offering of programmes will include sports holiday clubs, pub-style sports quizzes, sports clinics and camps. At the same time, the *Sports Outreach Resources Team* will develop Christian sports-related resources such as sports Bibles, booklets, games, prayer guides, DVDs and Christian sports magazines.

Working alongside the Interfaith/Multi-faith Committee, the *Chaplaincy Team* will assist in the recruitment of chaplains for the Religious Services Centre in the Athletes Village. They will also ensure incoming chaplains have suitable accommodation.

The *Community Festival Team* will set up community festivals in local parks and neighbourhoods. This is a fantastic opportunity for the church to re-insert itself into the community once again.

All programmes must have a Paralympic emphasis and the *Paralympic Team* will ensure churches are ministering to athletes and people with disabilities. Members of the *Creative and Performing Arts Team* will help celebrate our country's cultural diversity by encouraging churches to stage large- and small-scale concerts and performances.

There is also a darker side to any major sporting event. Research has found that sex-trafficking rises and that the homeless become marginalized when a city stages major sporting events. It is our role as Christians to reach out to the vulnerable. The *Social Justice Team* will involve local churches in projects combating these issues as well as promoting environmental awareness and Fairtrade.

Service teams – putting the love of Christ into action

The 2012 Games present a magnificent opportunity for churches and their members to show how the love of Christ leads to serving others. And an army of dedicated volunteers is vital if More Than Gold's extensive programme is to be delivered.

Staging the Games relies on thousands of volunteers, and the church can provide many committed men and women for this purpose. The *Volunteers Team* will encourage people to volunteer to work with the official local organizing committee

LOCOG to answer the need for helpers. Similarly, the *Torch Relay Team* will encourage churches to get involved with Olympic and Paralympic Torch Relay programmes as the torches cross the length and breadth of the country.

Meanwhile the *Canteen Operations Team* plans to provide spectators with a million cups of water, tea and coffee.

Hospitality teams – a generous welcome in Jesus' name

Genuine faith is always expressed through generous and welcoming hospitality. More Than Gold's aim is for the 2012 Games to be renowned for the level of hospitality offered to overseas visitors by the UK's Christians.

Through the More Than Gold hospitality programme, churches and their members can serve the athletes' families and the hundreds of thousands of visitors coming for the Games.

The *Athlete Family Homestay Team* will encourage Christians to host the families of Games athletes – providing a bed, breakfast and practical help for those who would otherwise miss seeing their relatives take part.

The *Service and Missions Team* will ask churches to host members of international mission teams coming to share their faith with visitors and serve the local church.

The *Hospitality Team* will encourage churches to run hospitality centres, which will show practical care to visitors, provide Internet access and provide welcome kits.

A Unique Opportunity

There are millions of people throughout the UK who might have their first experience of 'Church' when they participate in a big screen showing of the Opening Ceremony hosted by the local churches.

There are hundreds of thousands of spectators who might see for the first time a simple act of service when a church volunteer hands them a much needed drink of water. And there will be hundreds of athlete family members who would not be able to see their relatives compete without Christians being willing to host them for free.

There will be enormous media coverage with up to nine out of every ten people expected to watch some of the Games on television. Millions, of all ages, will avidly follow every huff, puff, spill and saga. This offers the local church a great way of impacting the lives of:

- Guests from around the globe – athletes, their families and international visitors.
- Those in their own community – children, youth and adults.

Most people see church as irrelevant and out of touch. Through the 2012 Games, churches, including yours, can tell a different story. They can be hosts of the biggest party the UK has seen for a lifetime.

Now the baton has been passed to the churches in the UK there is much that can be done.

1. Engage with people of all ages, especially youth and those normally hard to reach.
2. Serve your community through guest events, sports outreach and creative arts.
3. Work with other churches locally, nationally and internationally.
4. Make an international impact by partnering with a church from another country.
5. Increase the visibility and credibility of your church.

Thinking through the issues

To make the most of this once-in-a-lifetime opportunity, churches are encouraged to:

- **Start early** with talking, praying, planning and dreaming – late adopters will miss out on many opportunities.
- **Involve every section of the church** – youth and children, evangelism co-ordinators, teachers, mission committees, social responsibility activists and more.
- **Start with what is there already** – what is the church already doing that can be given an Olympic overlay? Alpha? Holiday clubs? Schools outreach? Guest services?
- **Identify how the local community is engaging** – and look for ways to join in rather than compete.
- **Appoint a Gold Champion** – the way for a church to make informed decisions about the 2012 Games and More Than Gold is by having their own Gold Champion/Church Representative who will receive their own dedicated eNews update, On Track, and invitations to special briefings. They will also be able to link with other Gold Champions in their area to share ideas, plans and opportunities. Registration, which is free, is at www.morethangold.org.uk/goldchampion.

Learning from past experience

Church leaders from the summer Olympics in Atlanta, Sydney, Athens and Beijing have all found that the above noted ideas gave them unique and cost-effective opportunities to serve, reach out and share the love of Christ to their local community as well as with the thousands of visitors. For example, in Atlanta over 3 million cups of water were distributed at Olympic venues to spectators, and over 2,000 athlete family members were hosted in church folks' homes. In Sydney, over 225,000 people watched the Opening Ceremony at big screen festivals co-ordinated by local churches. In Athens, over 20 tonnes of Bibles were distributed, and during the Beijing Games over 1,500 Service and Mission Teams made themselves available to serve the local church.

World Cup in South Africa

The response of South African churches to the World Cup clearly shows what can be done with a worldwide sporting event. Churches had taken the opportunities offered by Christian sports ministries like SCAS, Athletes in Action, Ambassadors in Sport and others, all co-ordinated under the South African Sports Coalition (SASCOL). In a similar way that More Than Gold is approaching the 2012 Games, the sports ministries in South Africa established 'The Ultimate Goal' and set out to train 2,000 churches, run sports-based outreach, reach 14 million people during the course of the World Cup and facilitate soccer outreach in 40 African countries.

'Not every goal was reached,' said David Willson, CEO of More Than Gold, 'but great things happened.' There were new levels of unity among churches and some fantastic outreach of communities and visitors. Even the smallest of churches were encouraged by being part of a thrilling movement and having access to many resources both material and personnel.

Training opportunities for festivals and schools games engagement

Plans are in hand to produce 'come and see' festivals and projects with large groups of young people. In various areas of the country 'Kids Games' will be up and running so that observers can learn from first-hand experience and then go away and set them up in their own regions and neighbour-hoods. Kids Games has been a universal phenomenon over the last decade, and the summer term of 2012 would then see UK Schools Games co-ordinated up and down the country, with the resolve to use the impetus created to develop it strongly over the years following.

Likewise, a number of churches around the country will be modelling Big Screen Community Festivals in their local communities around the FA Cup and Champions League Final. Training will also be provided at these events for churches wishing to learn from the experience.

There is no doubt that the true legacy of More Than Gold will be the structure and network that it leaves behind after the 2012 Games, both in London and throughout the UK. Certainly for sports ministry, the prospect of such a future foundation is quite breathtaking.

Models of Ministry During International Events

Four models of outreach have been consistently used over the past 30 years of major event ministry outreach. These models are:

1. Church Service Strategy
2. Sports Tournament
3. Outreach Meals
4. Big Screen Parties/Community Festivals

1. Church Service Strategy

During large international events it is recommended that every church has a More Than Gold worship service. The following ideas can help in the construction of such a service:

- Promote the More Than Gold service through all church communication channels.
- Decorate the foyer or the main body of the church with sports images to create a Games feel.
- Encourage the congregation and their friends to come in sports leisure wear.
- Select music that complements an upbeat service. Put significant words to a well-known sports tune.
- Include scripture that emphasizes the values related to sport and competition:
  - Philippians 3:14 'Press on towards the goal . . . '
  - Hebrews 12:1 'Run with perseverance the race . . . '
  - 2 Timothy 4:7 'I have finished the race . . . '
- Emphasize prayer which could include the following:
  - The sportspersons on the team in your country.
  - The Games – for a safe, crime-free event.
  - Any church outreach that is going on around the Games.
  - Organizations and individuals that are regularly seeking to share the good news of Jesus through sport.
- Present a sermon featuring sports or competition illustrations, using DVD or video clips where possible. Some sports-related Bible verses could give the basis to the sermon:

Mark 8:34–38	Winning through losing
1 Corinthians 9:24–27	Run to win
Ephesians 6:10–20	The right equipment
Galatians 6:9	Do not become weary
1 Timothy 4:7–8	In training
1 Timothy 6:11–12	Fight the good fight
2 Timothy 2:5	The victory crown

- 1 Peter 1:7   More Than Gold
- 1 Peter 1:13–16   Prepare for action
- 1 John 5:4b   Victory that overcomes
- Invite a local sportsperson to give a personal testimony on how their sport and Christian faith are a good mix.
- Have a More Than Gold resource table in the foyer of the church with tracts, books or booklets. Resources and information are found in plenty on the website www.morethangold.org.uk.
- Be prepared for the next step after this service:
  - Give details of a sports competition the church might be running.
  - Announce about the big screen party that has been planned.
  - Invite new people to a sports Alpha evening or something similar.
  - Have something lined up to do with men e.g. outdoor pursuits weekend.

2. Sports Tournament

Some people love to compete. A well-run tournament or competition will be very popular. While a competition in an individual sport like tennis is fine, there are advantages in the team-game competition since it involves more people, and people enjoy playing with friends and making new ones.

Football (soccer), basketball, netball or tag-rugby are excellent sports for such a competition. Choose a sport that will work in your area where you have the facilities and it is popular with the people you are trying to reach. It does not have to be an Olympic Games sport.

Purpose

Decide on the purpose of the event. It may be to present the gospel or it may just be to make initial contact with people who don't come to church. Once good relationships have been established then the next step can be considered.

Practicalities

Book a sports field or sports hall as appropriate. Make sure you have the necessary kit and equipment. Have competent officials (referees, umpires). Decide how many teams you want. Ideally a church member will invite a group of friends to play in his or her team.

Strategy

The aim is to run a competition which everyone enjoys playing. Arrange it so that every team plays at least twice. Avoid having too many teams and too long a gap between matches. At the end, present prizes and give out invitations to your next event.

Integrity of the event

Aim to run the event as professionally as you can. Don't in any way give the impression that sport is unimportant and only a means to the end by preaching to the captive audience. It is a way of serving the community with a well-thought-out and enjoyable competition.

Christian content

The prize giving ceremony at the end provides an excellent opportunity for some Christian content. Depending on your purpose, this can be either a gospel presentation or a more low-key invitation to the next event.

Materials

Give everyone involved in the competition a gift when they leave. More Than Gold has a number of resources that would fit this bill.

Follow-up

Where possible make the competition part of a programme of events, and always have some future events lined up to invite people to.

3. Outreach Meals

Opportunity

People enjoy eating! Inviting friends to a dinner is easy to do.

Purpose

The purpose is to have a pleasant time together and to share the gospel through an after meal speaker. If this is one of a series of events, it can be used to invite people who have been to a big screen presentation or a sports competition to a more formal presentation of the gospel. Make sure the evening is fun.

Practicalities

Book a venue – the church, a neutral venue like a hotel or sports club or a home. Arrange the menu. If the numbers are large enough then arrange a public announcement system. Book a speaker and brief them as to exactly what you expect.

Programme

Avoid the temptation to overcrowd the programme but be open to music, video, testimony and drama. Brief the speaker thoroughly as to exactly what you want (how long, how direct, the type of audience, etc.).

Materials

A gift can be given to people as they leave. Details of More Than Gold's resources are available on the website www.morethangold.org.

Follow-up

If possible make the meal part of a programme of events. Have some future event lined up to invite people to. Use attractive invitation cards.

Other points

Response cards can be used to gain feed-back and to identify people willing to be followed up. A seating plan can enable you to seat people strategically but may be too formal for what you are planning.

4. Big Screen Parties

Opportunity

The Olympic Games may be taking place in London but a large majority of people won't have a ticket to see the events first-hand. They will end up watching the Games on television. Over 85 per cent of the UK population watched the Beijing Games, so how much more fun would it be for them to watch it on a big screen with a crowd in a great atmosphere. Showing the Games events in partnership with other churches in a neutral venue can create an excellent opportunity for ministry to the local community.

Purpose

Decide on the purpose of the event. It may be to present the gospel. It may just be to make contact with people who do not come to the church and make friends with them.

Opening and closing ceremonies

All family members are interested in the ceremonies and this is an opportunity to provide a safe non-threatening outreach to one and all. People will enjoy meeting new friends and become acquainted with each other and with your church or organization. This brings the Games excitement home to many by allowing them a place to participate in the viewing of them with a sense of fun and community.

Practicalities

You need the technology (screen, TV, projector, etc.). You need a TV licence. The More Than Gold Festivals Team will provide you with a training manual and all the information you need to know to put on a big screen event either indoors or outdoors.

Strategy

The aim is to create the atmosphere of being at the game. Put flags or banners outside the venue. Have refreshments available, activities for the children, creative arts and sports competitions leading up to the screening of the event. It is important that the guests feel that they have genuinely been invited to participate in the event, rather than just attend an event that has been used to get them into a situation where they can be preached at.

Integrity of the event

Respect the integrity of the event. Do not make intrusive announcements or try to share the gospel at inappropriate times.

Added extras

For indoor broadcasts, some churches in the past have put more comfortable seats in part of the room and allowed people to reserve them in advance – like executive boxes in a stadium. Give everyone a small gift on arrival or departure.

Christian content

Depending on the purpose of the event, you may wish to include a presentation of the gospel in the programme. This can be done at a convenient break in the action or at the end

– although both can interfere with the integrity of the event. An alternative, which has worked successfully in the past, is to serve food first and then follow this by a Christian presentation before the sports event starts. The Christian content can be a live speaker or a video presentation. For some Big Screen Festival events, the fact that the church is putting on the event for free and serving the community is sermon enough.

Materials

Again, the More Than Gold website will be helpful with resources for this event.

Follow-up

If possible make the big screen presentation part of your programme of events. Always have some future event to invite people to and make sure to check out the new Sports Alpha course, available in the autumn of 2011.

In the lead up to the London Olympics, More Than Gold will be running their Vision Casting and Training Tours around the country in order to equip churches, organizations and individuals in their quest to reach their family, friends, neighbours and communities for Christ.

As the UK embarks on a decade of international sporting events in its own backyard – Olympics, Commonwealth Games, World Cup Rugby, World Cup Cricket – now is the time for the Christian community to emerge from its comfortable arena and 'play away' on the world's fields. The message of new life in Jesus is eternally unchanging and takes all who embrace it *beyond the gold*.